booksonline

Read this book online today:

With SAP PRESS BooksOnline we offer you online access to knowledge from the leading SAP experts. Whether you use it as a beneficial supplement or as an alternative to the printed book, with SAP PRESS BooksOnline you can:

- Access your book anywhere, at any time. All you need is an Internet connection.
- Perform full text searches on your book and on the entire SAP PRESS library.
- Build your own personalized SAP library.

The SAP PRESS customer advantage:

Register this book today at *www.sap-press.com* and obtain exclusive free trial access to its online version. If you like it (and we think you will), you can choose to purchase permanent, unrestricted access to the online edition at a very special price!

Here's how to get started:

1. Visit *www.sap-press.com.*
2. Click on the link for SAP PRESS BooksOnline and login (or create an account).
3. Enter your free trial license key, shown below in the corner of the page.
4. Try out your online book with full, unrestricted access for a limited time!

Your personal free trial **license key** for this online book is: 34qn-75wd-r2th-ipgj

ABAP™ Development for SAP® Business Workflow

SAP PRESS

SAP® Essentials

Expert SAP knowledge for your day-to-day work

Whether you wish to expand your SAP knowledge, deepen it, or master a use case, SAP Essentials provide you with targeted expert knowledge that helps support you in your day-to-day work. To the point, detailed, and ready to use.

SAP PRESS is a joint initiative of SAP and Galileo Press. The know-how offered by SAP specialists combined with the expertise of the Galileo Press publishing house offers the reader expert books in the field. SAP PRESS features first-hand information and expert advice, and provides useful skills for professional decision-making.

SAP PRESS offers a variety of books on technical and business related topics for the SAP user. For further information, please visit our website: *www.sap-press.com.*

Ginger Gatling et al.
Practical Workflow for SAP (2nd edition)
2009, 953 pp.
978-1-59229-285-1

Horst Keller, Sascha Krüger
ABAP Objects (2nd edition)
2007, 1059 pp.
978-1-59229-079-6

Horst Keller, Wolf Hagen Thümmel
Official ABAP Programming Guidelines
2009, 398 pp.
978-1-59229-290-5

Horst Keller
The Official ABAP Reference (3rd edition)
2012, 1688 pp.
978-1-59229-376-6

Ilja-Daniel Werner

ABAP™ Development for SAP® Business Workflow

Galileo Press

Bonn • Boston

Galileo Press is named after the Italian physicist, mathematician and philosopher Galileo Galilei (1564–1642). He is known as one of the founders of modern science and an advocate of our contemporary, heliocentric worldview. His words *Eppur si muove* (And yet it moves) have become legendary. The Galileo Press logo depicts Jupiter orbited by the four Galilean moons, which were discovered by Galileo in 1610.

Editor Patricia Kremer
English Edition Editor Laura Korslund
Translation Lemoine International, Inc., Salt Lake City, UT
Copyeditor Ruth Saavedra
Cover Design Nadine Kohl, Graham Geary
Photo Credit iStockphoto/johnnyscriv/5619393
Layout Design Vera Brauner
Production Graham Geary
Typesetting Publishers' Design and Production Services, Inc.
Printed and bound in Canada

ISBN 978-1-59229-394-0

1st edition 2012
1st German edition published 2011 by Galileo Press, Bonn, Germany

Library of Congress Cataloging-in-Publication Data
Werner, Ilja-Daniel.
[Workflow-Programmierung mit ABAP. English]
ABAP development for SAP business workflow / Ilja-Daniel Werner. — 1st ed.
p. cm.
Includes index.
ISBN-13: 978-1-59229-394-0
ISBN-10: 1-59229-394-8
1. ABAP/4 (Computer program language) 2. SAP ERP.
3. Management information systems. I. Title.
QA76.73.A12W4713 2012
005.13'3—dc23
2011020818

FSC
www.fsc.org
MIX
Paper from responsible sources
FSC® C011825

Contents at a Glance

Dear Reader,

Imagine a scenario in which you need something simple, such as a pencil. You fill out an order form, which is sent to the sales department, who sends it to the warehouse, who then sends you a pencil. You now have an example of workflow. For more complex situations than this, you have SAP Business Workflow, which is a tool that helps you design and run business processes in the SAP system.

With this book, Ilja-Daniel Werner shows you how to adapt and develop existing ABAP workflows for your individual business needs with concrete examples that are based on his expert experiences. Whether you are an ABAP developer or workflow expert, I am confident that this book will provide invaluable assistance in developing and expanding your knowledge and skills.

We appreciate your business, and welcome your feedback. Your comments and suggestions are the most useful tools to help us improve our books for you, the reader. We encourage you to visit our website at *www.sap-press.com* and share your feedback about this work.

Thank you for purchasing a book from SAP PRESS!

Laura Korslund
Editor, SAP PRESS

Galileo Press
Boston, MA

laura.korslund@galileo-press.com
www.sap-press.com

Contents

1 Introduction

First, I'd like to welcome you to the group of SAP Business Workflow programmers. This book evolved from the experience I've gained in my own workflow projects, as I'm originally an ABAP and Java programmer. As soon as you tackle a workflow project, "workflow-focused humanoids" suddenly bounce around the department using very strange vocabulary and have very unusual requirements for transportation dates, parameter design, quality assurance, and test scenarios. But they don't reveal exactly why these things are so important to them. After a fairly long time, these workflow people disappear, and it's now up to you to handle the ABAP part of the commissioned workflows. You might think this is not very difficult. But as soon as you change two or three totally harmless things, nothing works any longer. And that's when the workflow people appear again.

The special challenge in workflow programming is that the workflow-related ABAP development requires a somewhat different programming approach and you, as the developer, must understand the process knowledge. So you not only require special programming skills, but a very special process knowledge as well.

Motivation and Target Group

In this context, the modeling of new workflows is the most obvious "new territory," but it's not as difficult as it may seem to get used to the Workflow Builder and the various step types in the workflow. Literature, SAP online help, and of course SAP training (see Appendix A) are available for this purpose. Because I hold some of these training sessions myself, I'm aware of the gaps that exist between day-to-day ABAP programming and the training exercises. The goal of this SAP Essentials book is to attend to those gaps.

The difference between working with the Workflow Engine and using the classic application development is that different people execute their code in different roles. You must have multiple test users created in more complex workflows and examine your coding accordingly. Also, you must always ensure persistence, unique keys, and central logging—aspects whose importance is not as high as in "regular" ABAP programming.

This book is aimed at those who contribute to the workflow development and want to design their ABAP world to be maintenance-friendly and still "workflow-conscious." Of course, workflow modelers who want to take a close look at the ABAP side of workflow programming can find possible "starting points."

Content and Structure

In this book, you will get to know the Workflow Engine from the ABAP development perspective.

Initially, **Chapter 2**, Getting Started, deals with the workflow environment and how you can customize it. You learn how to find and examine sample workflows. Within the scope of this workshop, you can quickly determine the SAP Basis administrators in your team that you should see on a regular basis in future. Moreover, you are introduced to the maintenance of organizational structures that you require for agent determination.

Then **Chapter 3**, Compiling a Workflow Development Environment, presents the workflow development environment to give you a feel for the method of developing in the workflow environment. You learn how to navigate within the workflow components and keep track of your developed elements using a where-used list.

Chapter 4, Methods, Work Items, and Events, addresses and details the terms "work item," "methods," and "events" and the concepts behind these terms.

Chapter 5, Intervening in the Agent Determination, deals with the options that are available to influence the agent determination via the administration of responsibilities and programmed agent determination. As nice as a process may be modeled and as versatile as this model may be, it's also important that the right people are involved in a process. This programming activity is often underestimated in the workflow environment.

Even if a workflow is established in your operation, the people who are involved in this workflow presumably change more frequently than the workflow design itself. It's unacceptable that you or the workflow expert must be called whenever an employee is hired or transferred to a new department. The most powerful tool for this task is the organizational management borrowed from HR for the Workflow Engine. This means that as an ABAP programmer, you will still need to deal with this HR-related philosophy to some extent.

In Chapter 6, Containers, Binding, and Conditions in the Workflow, you learn how you can use ABAP programming to add additional features to the standard objects in the SAP Business Workflow. We give you detailed descriptions of the options that the workflow containers provide as a general data structure. Exercise examples describe the intervention in workflow processes (condition editor), binding, or event creation.

The last two chapters—**Chapter 7**, Sample Project—Designing an ABAP Objects Class for the Workflow, and **Chapter 8**, Sample Project—Designing a BOR Object for the Workflow—illustrate the development of concrete workflow objects. Based on identical core functionality, these chapters compile a workflow-enabled ABAP Objects class and a BOR object, respectively. The chapter discusses the specific features of BOR objects, such as enhancement, inheritance, and delegation, using a concrete example.

The appendices provide additional information: **Appendix A** lists all possible workflow steps and refers to sample workflows from the SAP standard that show their use. **Appendix B** summarizes the most important transactions for workflow programming in ABAP.

The entire presentation includes numerous figures and step-by-step instructions to help you implement your workflow requirements completely and deal with typical obstacles.

2 Getting Started

This chapter shows how you spend your first day with SAP Business Workflow. Our goal is to help give you a confident self-taught approach to the topic. Here you will get to know the requirements that are essential for the reliable operation of a workflow development environment. You will then learn about some workflows where you, as an ABAP programmer, may "copy" a little bit. Finally, you will create an organizational structure because the question "Who's the right one to do something?" plays a highly significant role in a business process.

2.1 Customizing the Workflow Engine

As you may imagine, the operation of the Workflow Engine requires some settings. This includes scheduling background processes for deadline and error monitoring, defining an administrator for the Workflow Engine, and much more. Let's discuss the essential aspects in the following subsections.

2.1.1 Implementing Customizing (Transaction SWU3)

When you start Transaction SWU3 (Automatic Workflow Customizing), if the system predominantly displays red crosses (indicating an incomplete customizing of the Workflow Engine), there are still a lot of things you need to do. Provided that you have the SAP_ALL authorization, click the IMPLEMENT AUTOMATIC WORKFLOW CUSTOMIZING ICON (, see Figure 2.1). Most of the little red crosses turn into small green checkmarks that tell you the Workflow Engine is satisfied with the most essential self-tests and that a functioning workflow runtime was reached.

If you don't have the SAP_ALL authorization, implement the automatic workflow customizing together with an administrator (see Section 2.1.2).

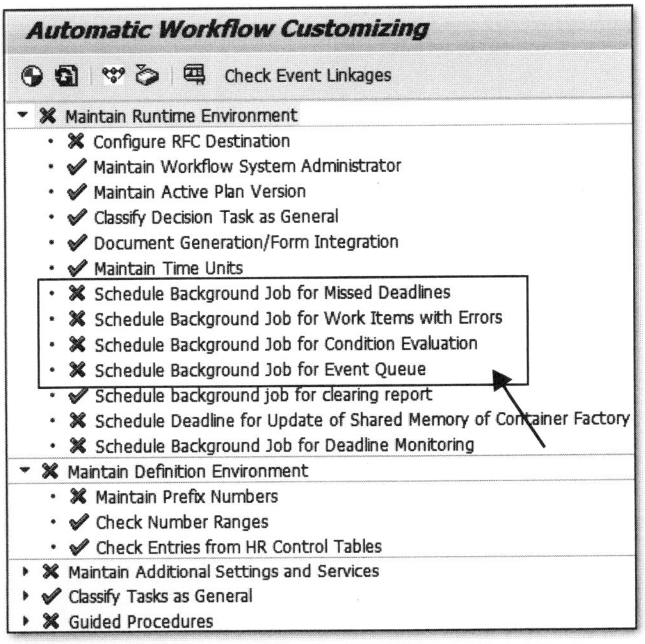

Figure 2.1 Transaction SWU3—Without Functioning Workflow Runtime

The system ensures that the steps that were already implemented are not started again, so you don't overwrite any Customizing settings when you restart the automatic workflow customizing later on. If the automatic workflow customizing encounters problems, you are provided with comprehensive notes that are helpful to read on the right-hand side of the screen in Transaction SWU3.

Following the automatic customizing, turn your attention to the individual subitems SCHEDULE BACKGROUND JOB FOR.... Select each step and read the information on the right-hand side. These background jobs (see the box *Memory Aid: Particularly Important Background Jobs* on page 23) are indispensable for the reliable operation of the Workflow Engine.

The customizing of a production or quality assurance system is completed when the Customizing categories MAINTAIN RUNTIME ENVIRONMENT and CLASSIFY TASKS AS GENERAL both appear with green checkmarks (see Figure 2.2).

In a workflow development system, you must also maintain the Customizing category MAINTAIN DEFINITION ENVIRONMENT so that only green checkmarks are displayed.

Figure 2.2 Transaction SWU3—With Valid Workflow Runtime and Valid Definition Environment

As a result of your work, you are now provided with a functioning workflow development system. The most important requirements for all examples presented in this book are thus set.

2.1.2 System User WF-BATCH

Because you usually use a workflow to model and automate business processes you can utilize through all functions of the SAP system, the Workflow Engine requires a user in whose context it executes the background steps. In the default version, this user is referred to as WF-BATCH and is of the `System` type. It has the SAP_ALL[1] authorization and is as important as the DDIC user. Because the WF-BATCH user

1 In fact, the WF-BATCH user inherits the authorizations of the user who initially executes Transaction SWU3, which is why an administrator with SAP_ALL rights should implement this task after each update or migration.

obtains an implicitly generated password and cannot log on to the dialog, it should not represent a security gap.

Renaming the WF-BATCH user or restricting the user's authorizations leads to side effects and error situations within the Workflow Engine, which impedes you as the developer. For example, the behavior of the background workflow tasks you've developed can massively differ from the behavior during your tests (that is, in the foreground) if the system user in the background (WF-BATCH) has fewer authorizations than you.

It therefore pays to insist on this special position for the WF-BATCH user even if enterprise-internal audits require that none of the users have the SAP_ALL authorization. Otherwise, you can refer to SAP Note 1251255 (Authorizations for System User WF-BATCH) to prepare for the consequences. This note refers to the authorization role SAP_BC_BMT_WFM_SERV_USER, which identifies the absolute minimum of authorizations for the WF-BATCH user.

Everything the Workflow Engine executes in the foreground; for example, from the *SAP Business Workplace,* runs with the authorizations of the user that starts such a *dialog work item*. However, each workflow step in the background runs as a *background work item* with the authorizations of WF-BATCH.

To enable the Workflow Engine to send emails in the background and convert Smart Forms into PDFs, you should set up an email address and a default printer for the WF-BATCH user.

2.1.3 Logical RFC Destination WORKFLOW_LOCAL_xxx

To change the user context, the communication with the Workflow Engine is done via an RFC destination with corresponding logon data. The RFC destination `WORKFLOW_LOCAL_xxx`[2] is created in Customizing for each client.

SAP Note 888279 provides further information on this RFC destination. Because you may start many workflows in a loop and these are not supposed to utilize all work processes of the SAP system, we recommend that you proceed as described in point 1 of SAP Note 888279 (Regulating the Workflow Load) at least in the development system and register the RFC destination `WORKFLOW_LOCAL_xxx` in the

2 `xxx` is the placeholder for the number of the client.

QOUT Scheduler (SMQS) and keep the number of connections for this destination below the number of dialog processes permitted in Transaction RZ12.

2.1.4 Checking the Customizing (Transactions SWU3 and SWUI_VERIFY)

The START VERIFICATION WORKFLOW icon in Transaction SWU3 provides the option to run an initial test of the Workflow Engine. A dialog box confirms the start of this verification workflow. The F1 help in this information dialog describes the subsequent steps (see Figure 2.3).

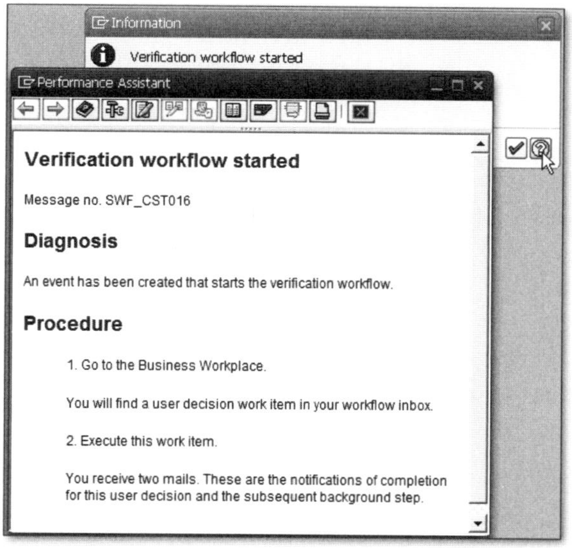

Figure 2.3 Explaining the Verification Workflow in the F1 Help

Within the scope of this initial test, the system takes you to the SAP Business Workplace (SBWP), which you can also reach via the corresponding icon in Transaction SWU3 (Automatic Workflow Customizing).

The SAP Business Workplace lists the executable work items under WORKPLACE • INBOX • WORKFLOW (see Figure 2.4).

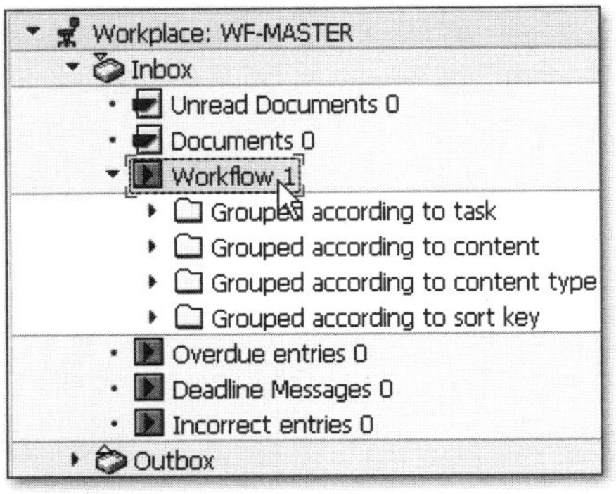

Figure 2.4 Transaction SBWP—Area with Executable Work Items

Select the First Step in Workflow Verification work item (see Figure 2.5). The system then displays a description of the work item on the lower right-hand side of the screen. Read the description and then execute the work item by double-clicking it.

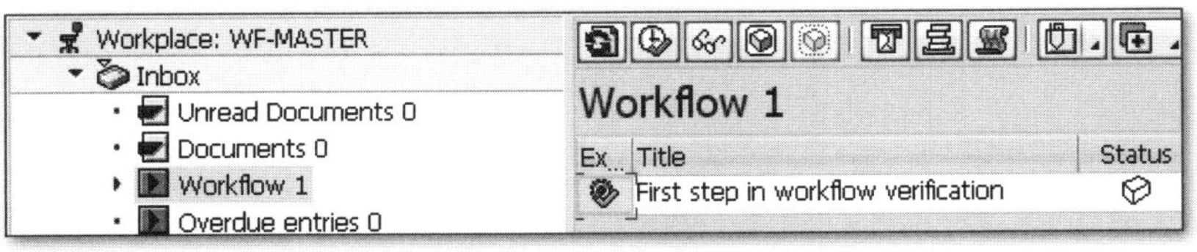

Figure 2.5 Transaction SBWP—First Work Item of the Verification Workflow Started in SWU3

In Figure 2.6, you can see a typical *decision task* with—in this case—three options.

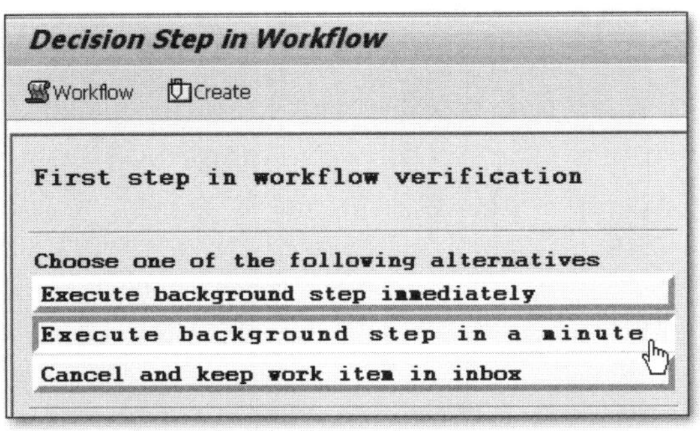

Figure 2.6 Decision Steps—Selection of One Option Required

Naturally, you can start the verification workflow multiple times and decide on a different option in each run. Examine the different behavior of the workflow that depends on the decision made.

Executed work items are removed from the inbox of the SAP Business Workplace, but they are still listed under WORKPLACE • OUTBOX • WORK ITEMS EXECUTED BY ME (see Figure 2.7).

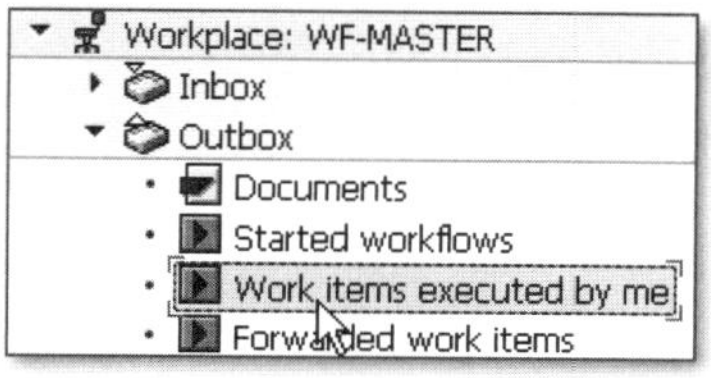

Figure 2.7 Transaction SBWP—Area of Work Items Already Executed

To obtain a more detailed technical view of this work item, reselect the work item and double-click it, or alternatively select the glasses icon to go to the view of executed work items. Besides the overview of the details on this work item, you also have the option here to navigate to the *workflow log* by clicking the LOG and GRAPHIC buttons (see Figure 2.8).

Figure 2.8 View of Executed Work Items—Navigation to the Graphical Log

You'll find the icon for the workflow log in various places; you can navigate to the log from many situations.

The *workflow log* is the central logging of the Workflow Engine. The first verification workflow discussed here is displayed either as a graphical log as shown in Figure 2.9 or as a technical log as shown in Figure 2.10.

Particularly in the initial phase, the graphical presentation of the workflow log can be very helpful. The benefit of this view is that it is very similar to the graphical development tool for workflows. A dotted line (which will appear as a green line in your actual screen) illustrates the path your workflow followed (not identifiable in Figure 2.9). You can get additional information by clicking or leaving the mouse pointer on the individual graphical elements.

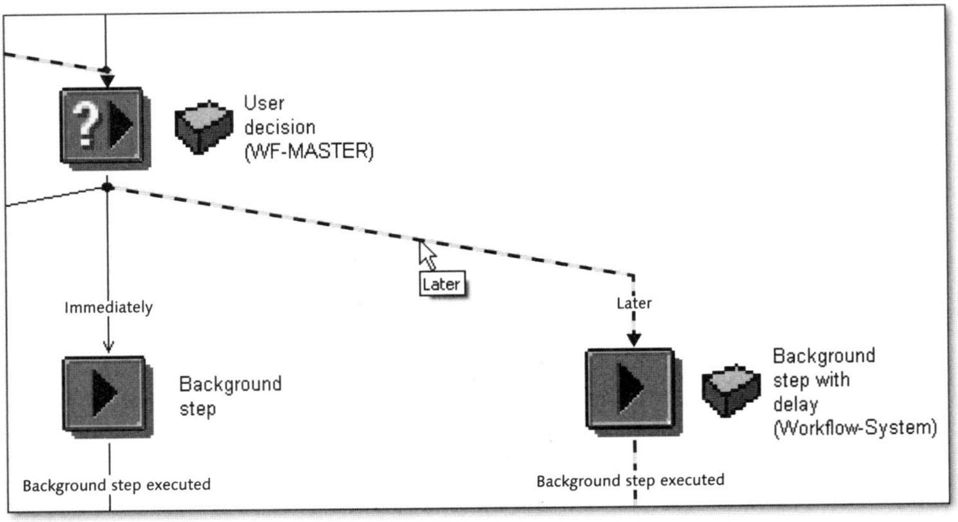

Figure 2.9 Graphical Presentation of the Workflow Log

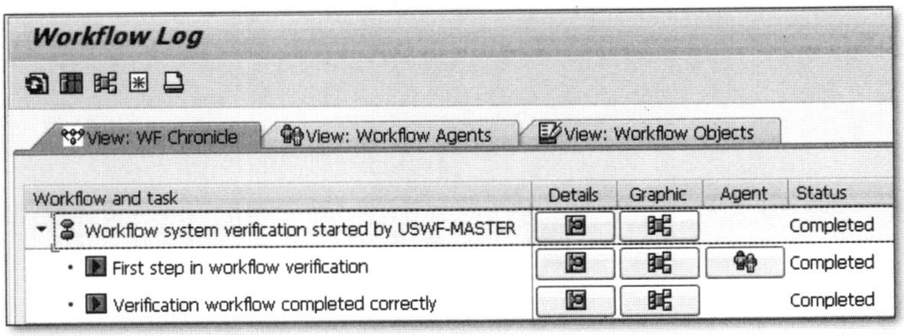

Figure 2.10 Technical Presentation of the Workflow Log

However, you will soon prefer the technical logs of a workflow to the graphical presentation because they present the information in a more compact form. You can easily determine that the graphical presentation (the green path) decreases in significance in a workflow with loops and branches; that is, with increasing complexity of the workflow template.

After this first successful workflow, you should concern yourself with another verification workflow, which is available via Transaction SWUI_VERIFY (Start Test Workflows). As an ABAP developer, you can surely find some interesting examples in this list. Execute them and frequently check the workflow log if possible. This way you can get an impression of how your Workflow Engine ticks.

The customizing of the Workflow Engine is definitely interesting for ABAP programmers.

Memory Aid: Particularly Important Background Jobs

Familiarize yourself with the classic ABAP techniques for asynchronous function calls via tRFC and qRFC:

- `SWWCOND`: Work item rule monitoring
- `SWWDHEX`: Work item deadline monitoring
- `SWWERRE`: Work item error monitoring
- `SWWCLEAR`: Clearing tasks in the workflow system

2.2 Starting Workflows and Monitoring the Workflow Events

After you've completed the preparations for the Workflow Engine operation, you can take a closer look at a demo workflow. Let's use the already known Transaction SWUI_VERIFY as the starting point (see Figure 2.11). The workflow template available there tests the Workflow Engine and dispenses the mapping of an organizational structure to the greatest extent.

So in the following business process example, you as the *workflow initiator* initially receive all work items. This is the user who manually started a workflow template or in whose user context the starting event was executed for the workflow template.

The procedure according to which the Workflow Engine determines the users to which a work item is sent is referred to as *agent determination*. For now, let's only discuss the workflow initiator, as this is always the SAP user who executes the test transaction or has generated the relevant event.

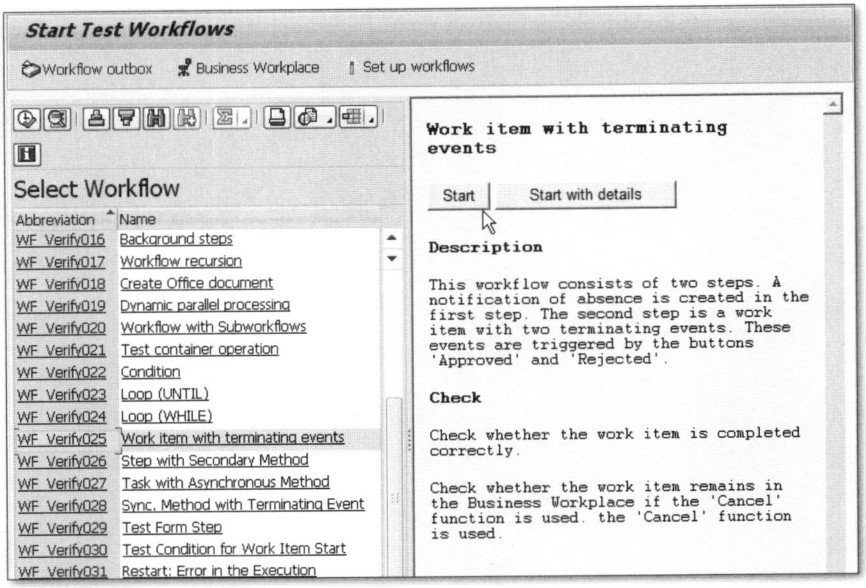

Figure 2.11 Transaction SWUI_VERIFY—Many Test Options for the Workflow Engine

2.2.1 Monitoring Events (Transactions SWELS and SWEL)

A business process may take a long time. During a business process, you can stop and restart the SAP system. To prevent the Workflow Engine from being caught in innumerable background loops, SAP has put great emphasis on persistence and asynchronous processing.

To design such an asynchronous processing robustly, special importance is attached to the delivery of events—nothing is supposed to "get lost."

1. Use the event trace to monitor which events are created in the system and how they are delivered to the Workflow Engine. Switch on the general event trace in Transaction SWELS (Switch Event Trace On/Off) (see Figure 2.12).

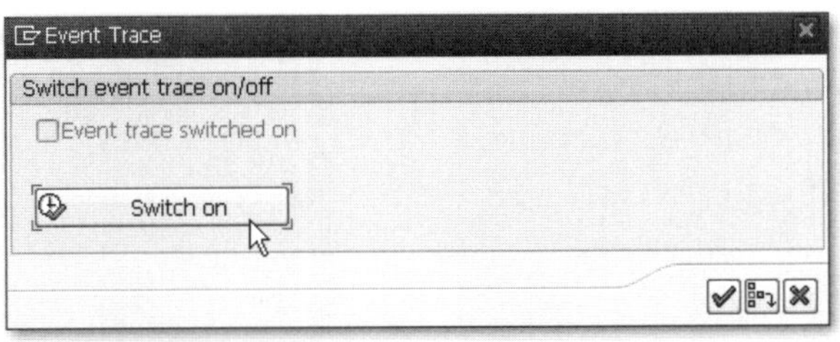

Figure 2.12 Transaction SWELS—Switching on the Event Trace

2. Return to Transaction SWUI_VERIFY and successively start the workflow templates `WF_Verify025` (see Figure 2.13) and `WF_Verify048` (see Figure 2.14).

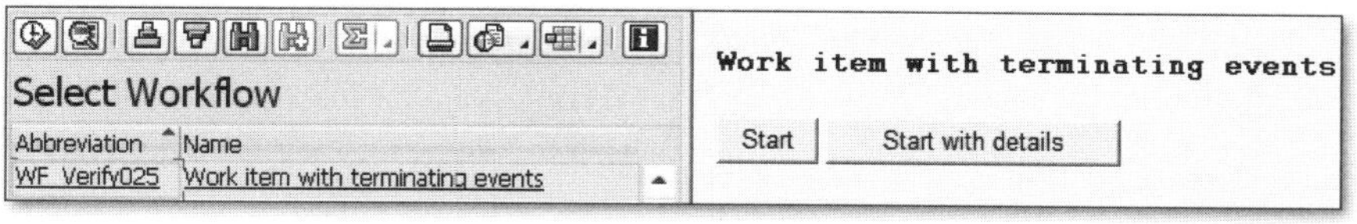

Figure 2.13 Workflow using a BOR Object for Notification of Absence Demonstrating Terminating Events

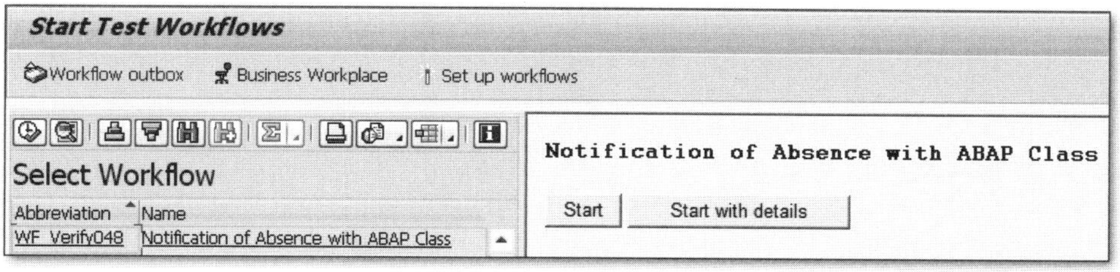

Figure 2.14 Workflow using an ABAP Class for Notification of Absence

Both workflows record the notification of absence of an employee in a simple form and submit this form for inspection or approval to another employee.

3. Follow the instructions for the implementation of the test and sample workflows, which are displayed on the right-hand side of the screen, as accurately as possible. During this test, you will come across several possible behaviors of a work item:

   - At one point, you must go to the SAP Business Workplace.
   - At another point, the Workflow Engine analyzes whether the work item is intended for the user whose SAP GUI instance is currently active. If this is true, the form is displayed automatically. This procedure is referred to as *advance in dialog* and is frequently used in test, training, and demo workflows. In more complex workflows that model comprehensive business processes, this procedure is rarely used.
   - At yet another point, you are prompted to complete the work item. This *explicit completion* can make sense if multiple comprehensive user actions are expected in a workflow step and the system cannot exactly determine based on events whether the prerequisites for continuing the workflows are

met. Here, the acting user must confirm explicitly that the workflow step is complete (see Figure 2.15).

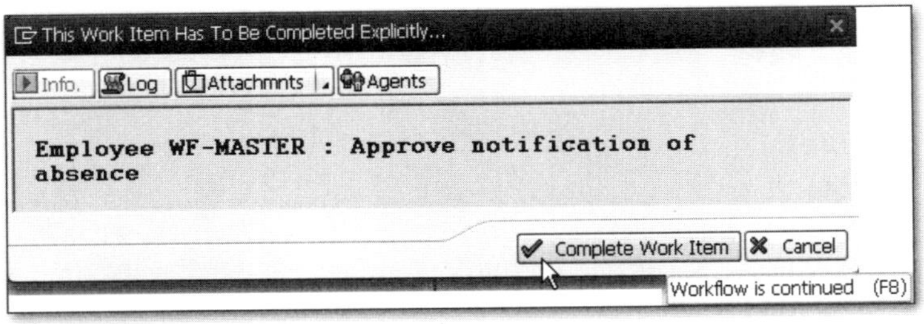

Figure 2.15 Explicit Completion of a Work Item

4. After you've passed the test workflow, go to Transaction SWEL (Display Event Trace) and select the events for object type `*FORM*`. You should now see the entries for `FORMABSENC` (a BOR object) and `CL_SWF_FORMABSENC` (an ABAP Objects class or ABAP OO class) (see Figure 2.16).

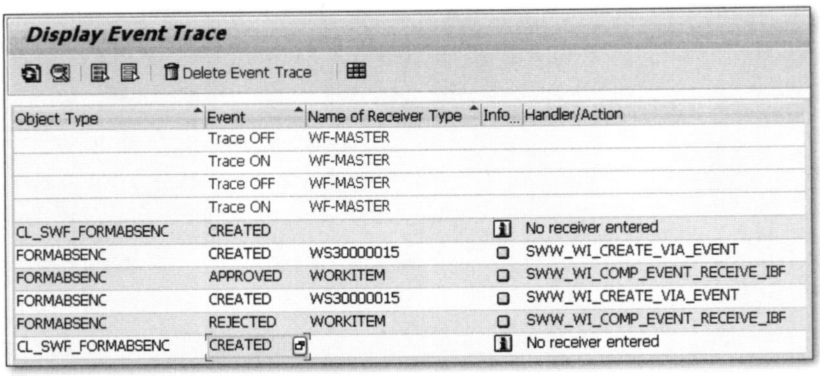

Figure 2.16 Events in the Event Trace—BOR Objects and ABAP Classes as Object Type

Workflow-relevant events can be triggered both by ABAP classes (identified by `CL_` in the name) and by BOR objects. For now, you only need to remember that these two object types exist.

You now know one of the most important analysis tools of the workflow development. If a workflow is not started, the triggering event is usually not created either.

Now switch off the event trace in Transaction SWELS again so the system doesn't write too much unnecessary information to the tracing tables (see Figure 2.17).

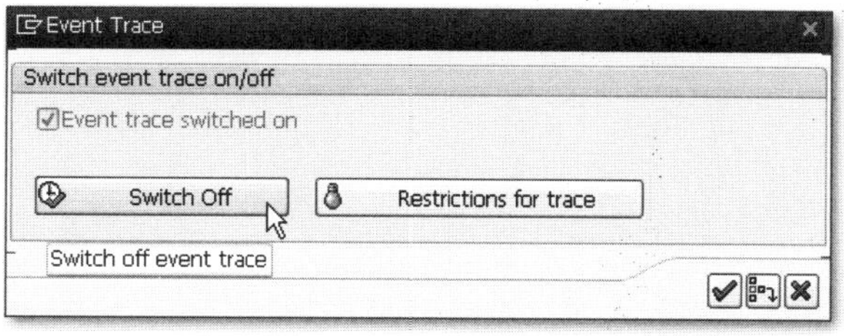

Figure 2.17 Transaction SWELS—Switching Off the Event Traces

The delivery of events can also depend on other criteria. For example, if an event is supposed to start a workflow only under specific conditions or if different workflows are to be started depending on the parameters of an event, special ABAP function modules are used.

Memory Aid: General Information on Workflows and Events

Remember the following:

- Objects the Workflow Engine uses—whether ABAP classes or BOR objects—are all programming-intensive elements.
- Events can be created directly using ABAP code.
- The delivery of events and the selection of the correct workflow can be influenced via ABAP.

2.2.2 Considering Workflow Definitions (Transaction SWDS)

In the previous section, we introduced an initial impression of the interaction of events and workflows. But how do you obtain an overview of the actual processes within a workflow?

The context menu of Transaction SWUI_VERIFY provides the option to go to the graphical presentation of the workflow template.

1. For this purpose, right-click a selected workflow template to open the context menu, and then select Display Workflow Definition (see Figure 2.18).

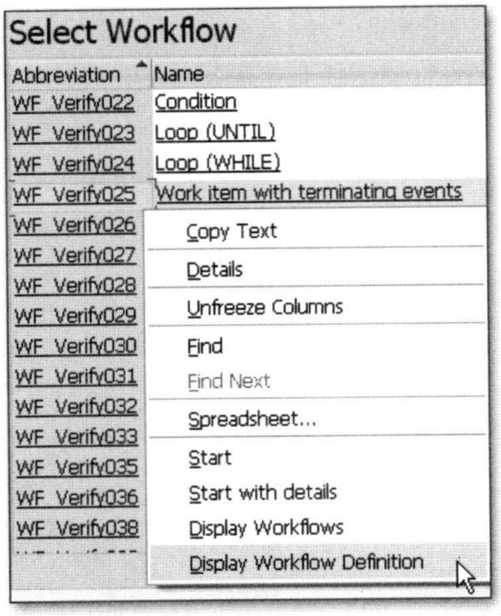

Figure 2.18 Transaction SWUI_VERIFY—View a Workflow Template Via the Context Menu

The function for the workflow display in Transaction SWDS (Workflow Builder) has the same effect.

2. In the Select Workflow dialog, for simplified selection enter the abbreviation of the workflow template under Task, and then press `Enter` (see Figure 2.19).

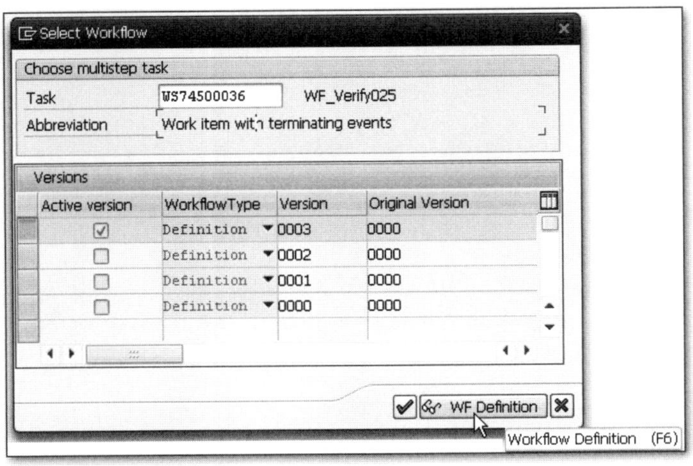

Figure 2.19 Transaction SWDS—Selection Screen

3. The system takes you to the quick view of the workflow definition of an existing workflow template (see Figure 2.20). You are already familiar with a similar view from the graphical workflow log.

However, the selection screen of Transaction SWDS (see Figure 2.19) already reveals a specific feature of the workflow development: Various versions of a workflow template can exist in the system, but only one of them is active. The idea behind it is that an already started workflow is supposed to run with the version of the workflow template with which it was started. If a new version of the template is created and activated while the business process is still running, this "update" is not supposed to lead to incompatibilities. New workflows are started with the new version of the workflow template. Old workflows continue with the old version until they are completed.

All blue boxes in the graphical presentation of a workflow template (see Figure 2.20) represent individual workflow steps.

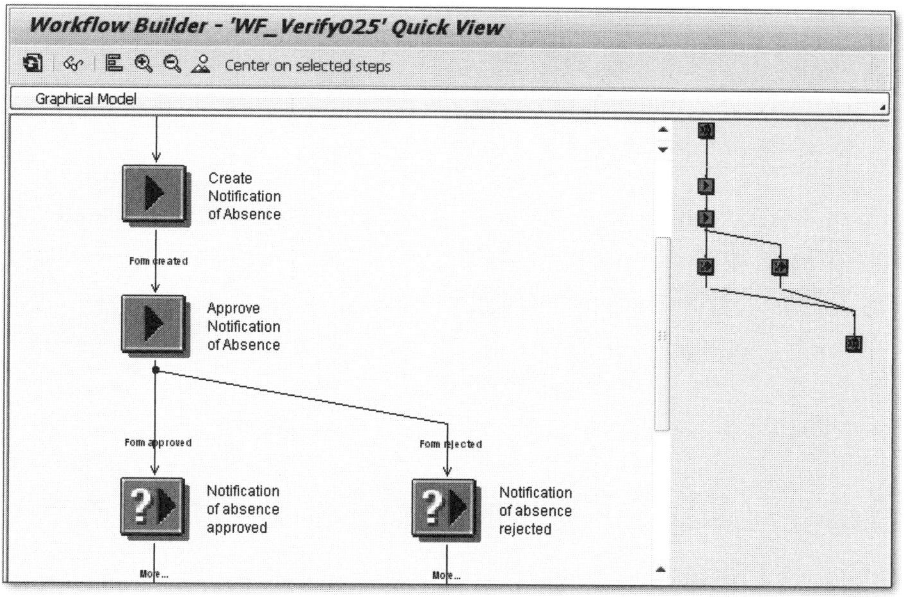

Figure 2.20 Graphical Display of the Workflow Definition

Here you can immediately recognize the philosophy of the Workflow Engine: An individual, reusable workflow step can be defined as a *standard task* and used in various workflow templates. In this example, various business processes can result in a notification of absence being entered. This could be required both in a vacation workflow and in a business trip or training workflow.

If you want to obtain further information on a workflow step, you can double-click it to navigate to the definition. Select the Approve Notification of Absence step as an example (see Figure 2.21).

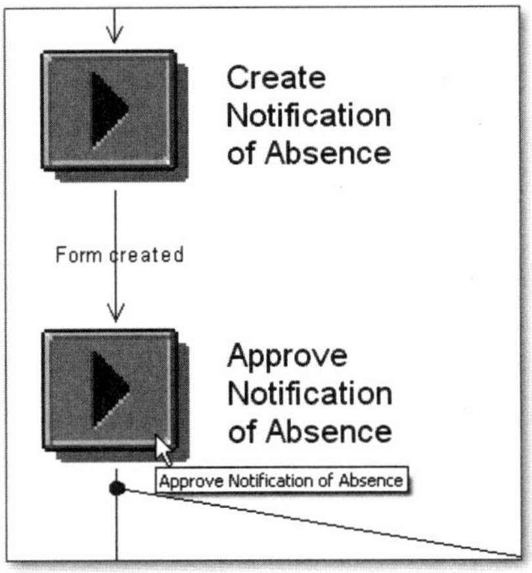

Figure 2.21 Navigating to an Individual Workflow Step

Besides other information, Figure 2.22 shows that in this workflow template the workflow step Approve Notification of Absence has the internal ID 24 and is implemented by standard task TS74507936.

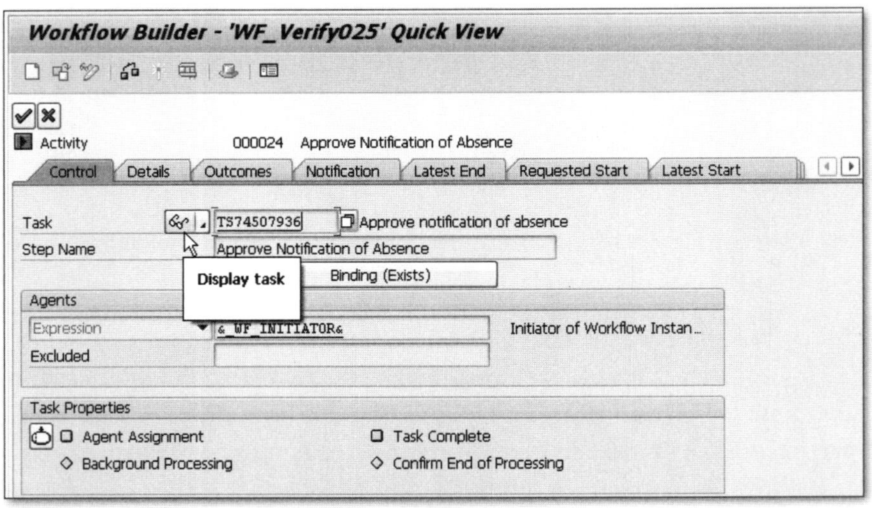

Figure 2.22 Workflow Step "Approve Notification of Absence"

On the CONTROL tab, click on the glasses icon next to the task number in order to navigate to the standard task's details.

On the BASIC DATA tab, you can see that the ABAP functionality for this step is provided by the APPROVEASYNCHRON method of the FORMABSENC BOR object (see Figure 2.23).

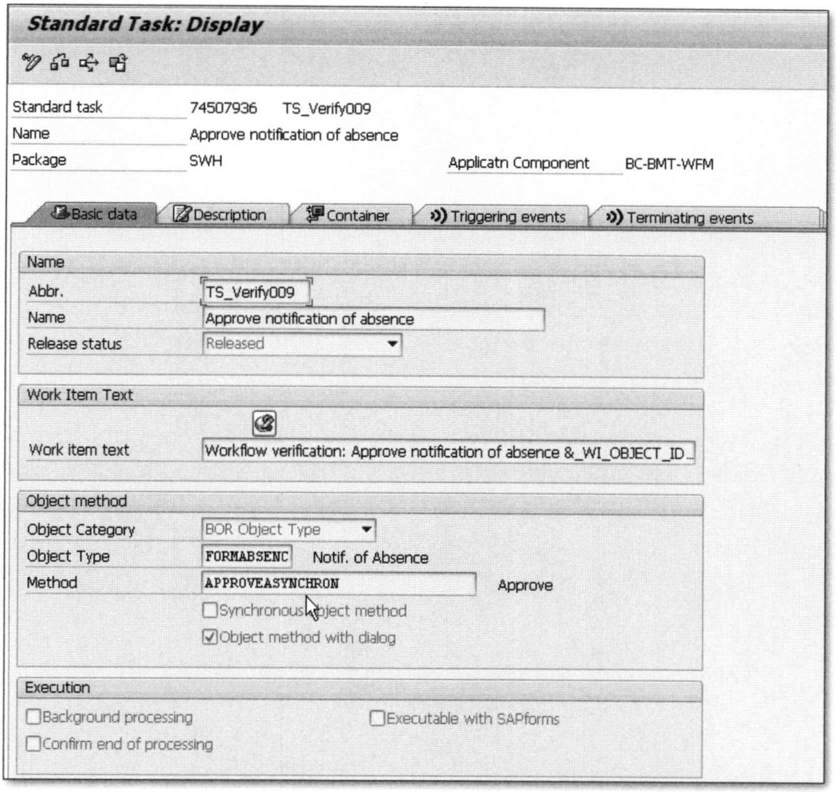

Figure 2.23 Basic Data of the Standard Task for Approving a Notification of Absence

According to the TERMINATING EVENTS tab, this standard task is terminated by the standard events FORMABSENC-APPROVED and FORMABSENC-REJECTED. You've seen at least one of these events in the event trace (see Figure 2.24).

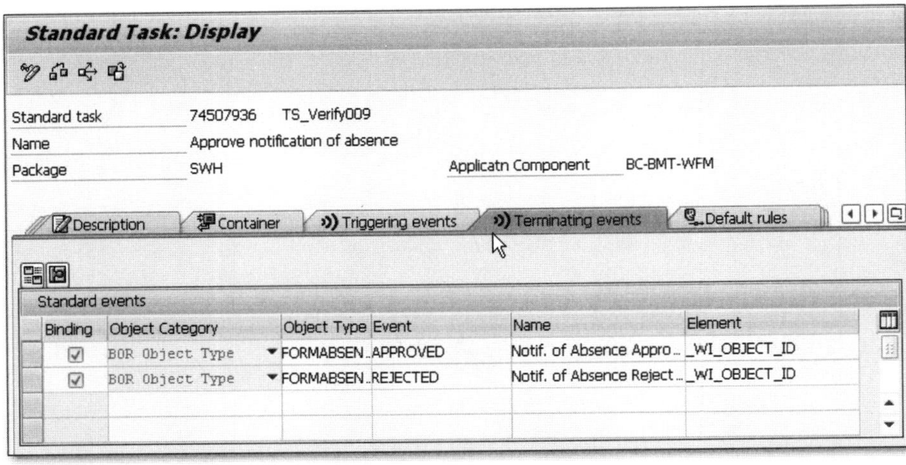

Figure 2.24 List of Events that Can Terminate the Standard Task

These examples illustrate that only the process flow itself is modeled in a workflow template. The actual SAP functionality is bundled by BOR objects or ABAP classes.

Memory Aid: Binding

Remember the following:

- You can influence how the data is transported from the workflow to the BOR objects and ABAP classes in the ABAP programming.
- The variables displayed in the work item text are based on BOR attributes. You can program them in ABAP in such a way that they are not calculated until they are queried.

2.3 Maintaining a Minimal Organizational Structure

Genuine business processes comprise a myriad of users and departments. Let's use a notification of absence as an example: There's the person placing the request, his departmental supervisor, and possibly the HR department (human resources).

Therefore, you cannot avoid summarizing and managing all of these participants of a workflow in some way or another.

Because every SAP system includes the control tables of SAP ERP Human Capital Management (HCM) and because SAP ERP HCM is a very powerful tool for managing such organizational structures, it is a good idea to build a little organizational structure—a "demo enterprise"—for the development of a workflow using a few SAP ERP HCM utilities. This organizational unit is the prerequisite for the subsequent examples of agent determination.

2.3.1 Creating Organizational Units (Transaction PPOCW)

First, you create your demo enterprise as an organizational unit. You then subordinate two departments to this organizational unit. Initially, a technical and a commercial department are sufficient. Departments represent organizational units.

1. Open Transaction PPOCW (Organization and Staffing (Workflow) Create). The system prompts the validity period of the organizational unit to be created; confirm the default settings (see Figure 2.25).

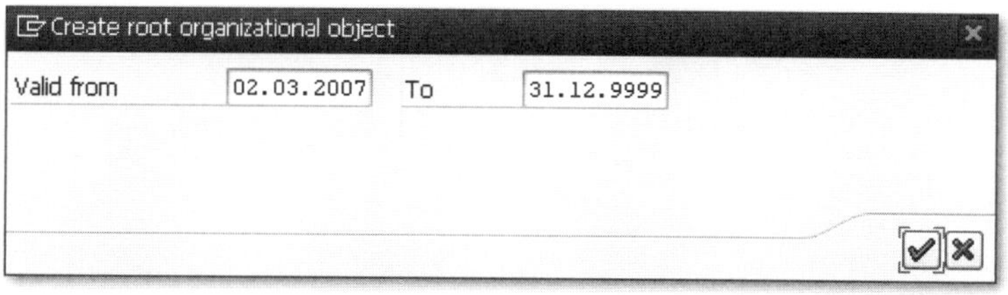

Figure 2.25 Time-Based Delimitation of Organizational Objects

Figure 2.26 shows the basic structure of transactions for organization maintenance. Because these transactions are borrowed from the SAP ERP HCM component (SAP's HR solution), ABAP programmers may have to get used to its handling. There are four main areas:

- **Search area** ❶
  Here you select areas of the organizational structure using search terms. They are displayed in the results area.
- **Results area** ❷
  (HIT LIST) Here you find the selection results according to the criteria entered in the search area. When you double-click a search result, the system displays the organizational element in the display area.

- **Display area** ❸
  Here you find the substructure of the organizational hierarchy you selected in the results area. Provided that this hierarchy has subelements, these are also displayed hierarchically.

- **Detail area** ❹
  (DETAILS FOR ORGANIZATIONAL UNIT NEW ORGANIZATIONAL UNIT) When you double-click an element in the display area, the system displays the relevant details of the organizational object.

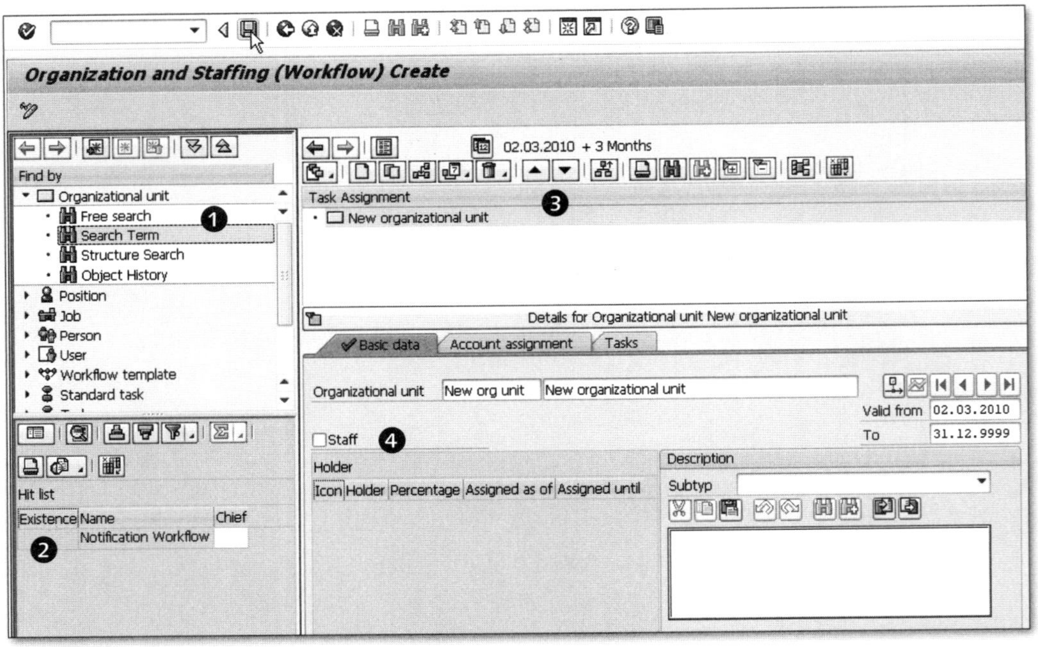

Figure 2.26 Typical Structure of Transactions for Organization Maintenance

2. Enter a technical abbreviation and a name for the new organizational unit in the detail area in the BASIC DATA tab (here ZDEMO_COMP "WF Demo Root Organizational Unit"), and save this new organization unit (💾 icon).
3. Create the technical and commercial department as a suborganization of your root organization. To do so, select the root organization and then select CREATE in the context menu (see Figure 2.27).

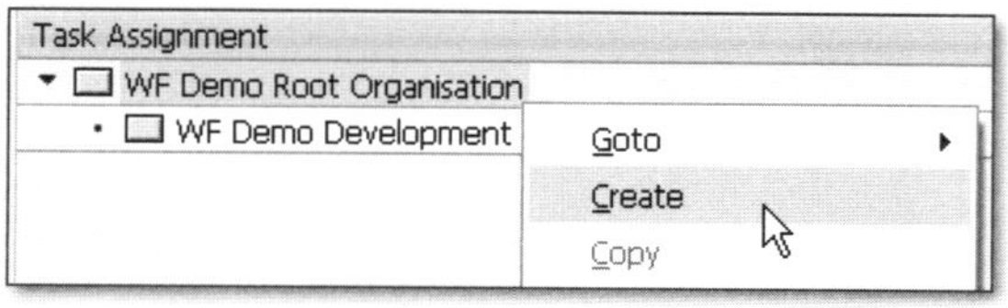

Figure 2.27 Creating Subobjects via the Context Menu

4. Because you want to create subsections; that is, further organizational units, select Is LINE SUPERVISOR OF in the subsequent screen (see Figure 2.28); later, you'll also add positions.

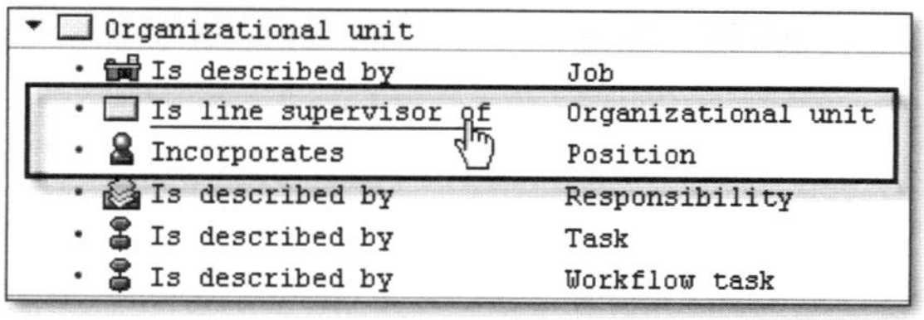

Figure 2.28 Organizational Units and Positions as Subobjects

5. Repeat this step to create two subordinate organizational units of the root organization:
   - ZDEMO_EDV "WF Demo Development"
   - ZDEMO_FI "WF Demo Sales"

Your demo enterprise should look like the screen shown in Figure 2.29.

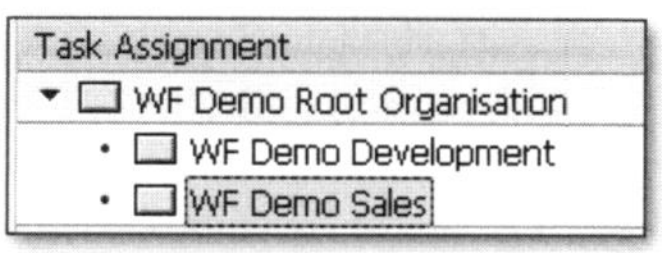

Figure 2.29 Organizational Hierarchy of a Sample Enterprise

You have now roughly defined the hierarchy of a demo enterprise.

2.3.2 Editing Organizational Units (Transaction PPOMW)

To ensure that the work items of a workflow in SAP Business Workplace reach "real" SAP users, you must now fill the organizational units of your demo enterprise with contents.

It's common HR practice to maintain at least two positions in every organizational unit: One for the person responsible in this department from the hierarchical point of view, and one for the other members of this department.

Transaction PPOMW is intended for processing organizational units that have already been created in the workflow. Open this transaction, and click on ORGANIZATIONAL UNIT under FIND BY (see Figure 2.30).

If you enter "ZDEMO*" or parts of the description of the previously created organizational units as the search term, you can restrict the search.

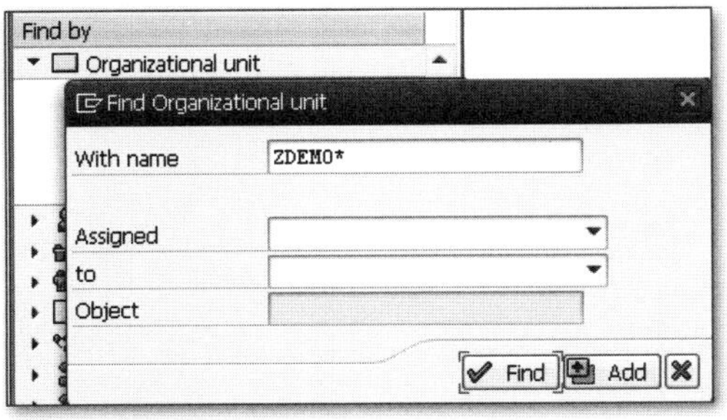

Figure 2.30 Search for Organizational Units

You should get exactly three hits in the results area:

- WF DEMO ROOT ORGANIZATION
- WF DEMO DEVELOPMENT
- WF DEMO SALES

Double-click the root organizational unit in the hit list. The display area should now look like the screen shown in Figure 2.29. To ensure that a subordinate organizational unit comprises a position, click it and select CREATE in the context menu (right-click).

Because you want to create positions, select the INCORPORATES entry to the left of the POSITION entry (see Figure 2.31).

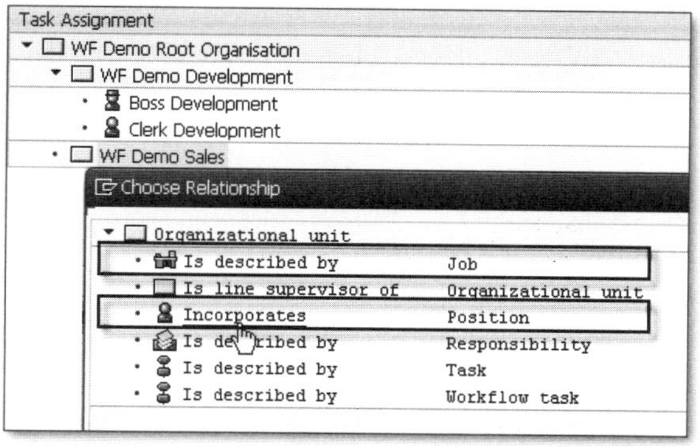

Figure 2.31 Adding Positions to Organizational Units

Create four positions:

- **In the organizational unit of the development department:**
  - ZDEMO_E_BOSS "Boss Development"
  - ZDEMO_E_USR "Clerk Development"
- **In the organizational unit of the commercial department:**
  - ZDEMO_F_BOSS "Boss Sales"
  - ZDEMO_F_USR "Clerk Sales"

To ensure that a position is identified as a supervisor in the HR sense and displayed with the icon, select the HEAD OF OWN ORGANIZATIONAL UNIT checkbox, as shown in Figure 2.32.

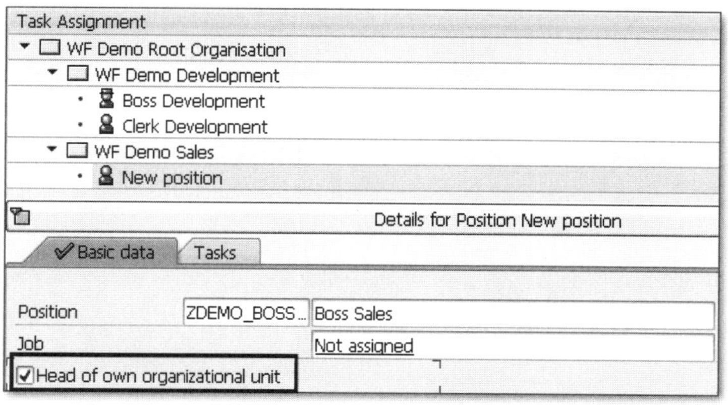

Figure 2.32 Positions for Supervisors and Employees

You have now defined the hierarchy of a demo enterprise.

2.3.3 Assigning SAP Users to Positions

Business processes and department hierarchies are decoupled from the actual SAP users with good reason; after all, a business process should not depend on individual users for the following reasons:

- Users and employees may change to another department or leave the enterprise.
- Technical processes are supposed to survive a restructuring of the enterprise.

All of this should affect the Workflow Engine to a limited extent only. It would incur unnecessary costs if every change to the employee structure resulted in changes to the workflow templates. The organizational hierarchy therefore assigns positions to the SAP users.

If possible, you should only use positions in your workflow templates. Later in this book, you'll learn how to link positions with jobs. This additional level of abstraction allows for a "cross-departmental" delivery of work items.

To occupy positions with SAP users, you use Transaction PPOMW again.

By double-clicking the USER icon ( ) in the search area you can create a hit list for SAP users, as illustrated in Figure 2.33.

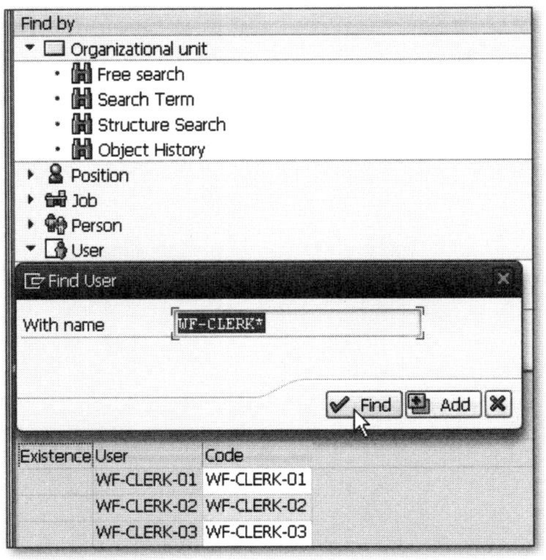

Figure 2.33 Transaction PPOMW—Search For SAP Users

The WF-CLERK* and WF-MGR* users exist in many SAP installations. These are now used for employees or supervisors. These users are usually used for SAP training and demonstrations.

If these users do not exist in your development system, have your SAP Basis team create some similar users, if required, by copying existing users.

When you develop a workflow template for mapping a real business process, you ideally create copies of real SAP users to be able to examine their authorizations more closely.

Now occupy all of your positions in your demo enterprise with at least one SAP user. The easiest way is to drag and drop a user from the hit list to the corresponding position (see Figure 2.34).

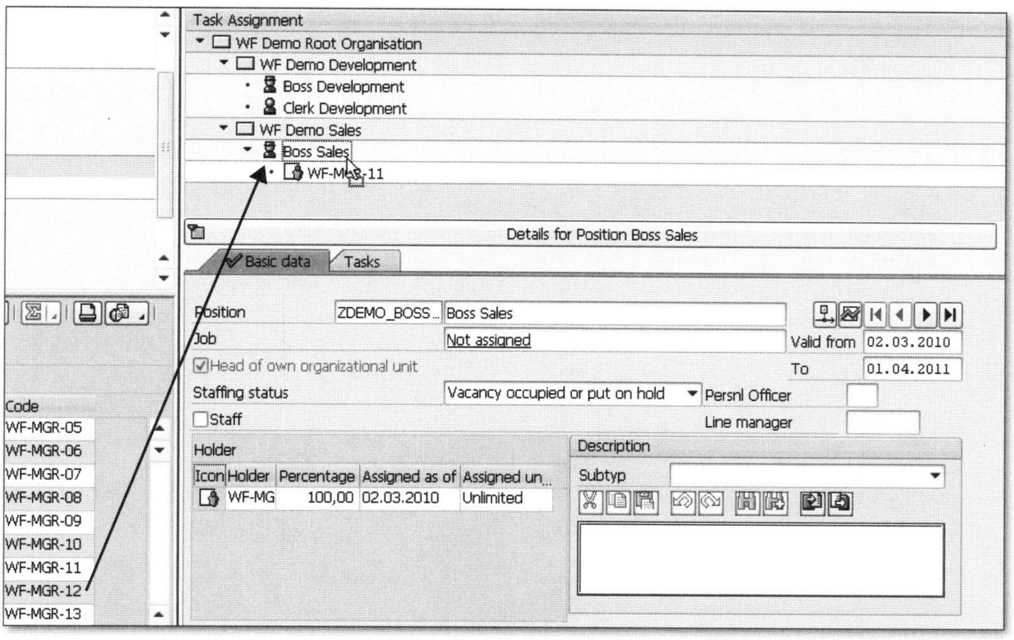

Figure 2.34 Assigning Users to Positions via Drag-and-Drop

You have now assigned SAP users to the positions in your enterprise and can thus assign work items to a position or organizational unit.

2.3.4 Testing the Agent Determination (Transaction PFAC)

To ensure that work items are assigned to an agent, you can either use a variable (an "expression") or rules. In large organizations, the selections in the SAP ERP HCM tables are elaborate. To save yourself from having to browse the entire organizational hierarchy in each workflow step, a large part of this hierarchy is buffered in the memory.

If you want to immediately test your newly maintained demo enterprise, you must re-import this buffer.

1. This is done via Transaction SWU_OBUF (Refresh Organizational Unit). Go to this transaction and force the synchronization of the organizational hierarchy's buffer (see Figure 2.35).

Figure 2.35 Transaction SWU_OBUF—Refreshing the Runtime Buffer for the Workflow

2. To maintain a rule for the agent determination, go to Transaction PFAC. Take a look at rule 00000157, which shows the hierarchically superior users via the chief position (see Figure 2.36).

Figure 2.36 Transaction PFAC—Displaying Rule 00000157

3. The system shows a rule that is based on the `RH_ACT_LEADING_POSITION` function module (see Figure 2.37).

You can reach the test tool for rules via the SIMULATE icon ().

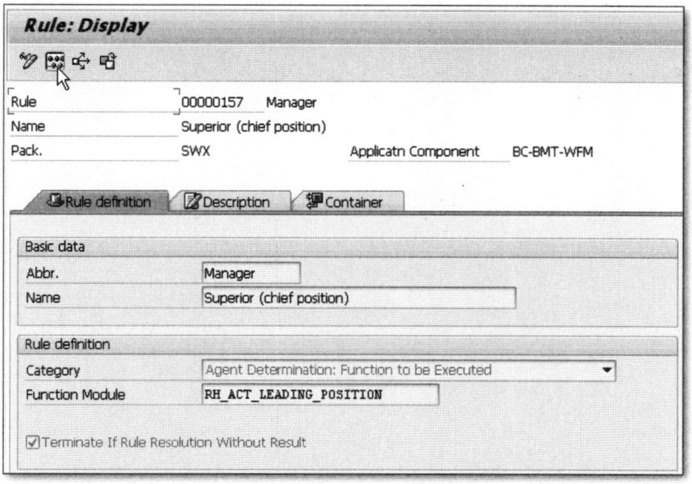

Figure 2.37 Simulating Rule 00000157

When you enter a user—consisting of the object type US and the user name—under AGENT in this simulation dialog window (see Figure 2.38), rule 00000157 determines the hierarchically superior organizational structure using the function module specified.

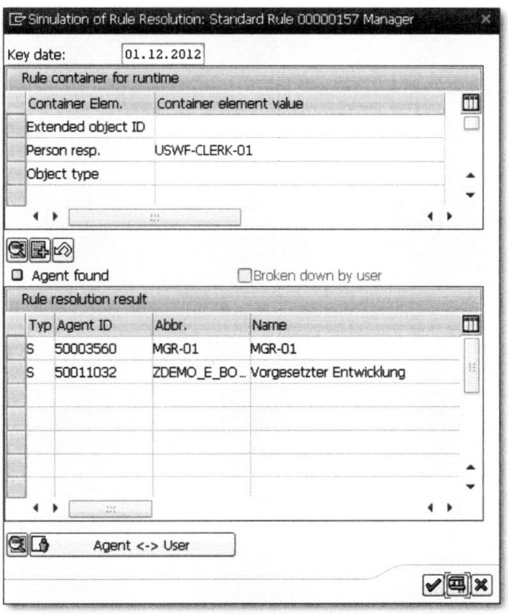

Figure 2.38 Rule 00000157—Result of the Simulation

After you've entered the agent, click the EXECUTE TEST icon () to run the test.

Because a user can be linked several times in the organizational structure, you can also determine several structures as the result, as is the case in this example.

To resolve these structures and display the individual SAP users, click the AGENT <-> USER button. Consequently, the test environment for rules determines a total quantity of users for which duplicates were removed and which are defined in the determined organizational structures (see Figure 2.39).

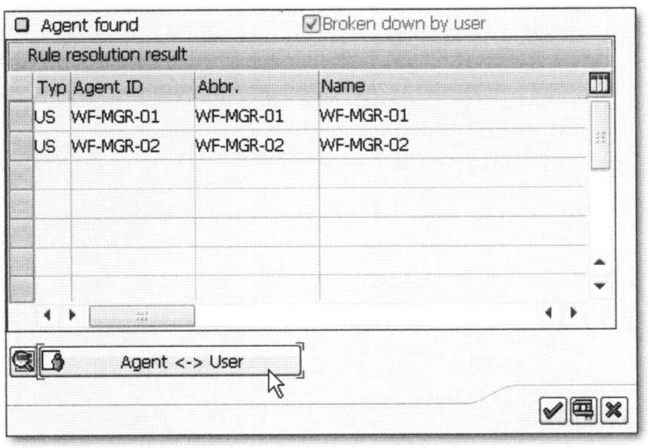

Figure 2.39 Simulation Result—Resolved by Users

The definition of the agent determination is a work step that ABAP programmers should not underestimate. In cooperation with the people involved in the process design, you must provide a corresponding development to ensure that there are no dialog work items without agent determination. Keep in mind that sensitive data can also be displayed in work item texts. Nobody wants to assume responsibility if the work item for approving your pay raise or for checking a personnel appraisal is accidentally sent to the entire enterprise.

Memory Aid: Agent Determination

Remember the following:

- Rules for agent determination are often based on newly defined links in the workflow-relevant organizational tables. Defining and selecting new links is a frequent ABAP task.
- The function modules for agent determination require a specific interface and a debug strategy that can only be controlled by ABAP programmers.

3 Compiling a Workflow Development Environment

Once you have configured the runtime environment of the Workflow Engine in all SAP systems, you can turn to the transactions you will use on a regular basis in your everyday work. This chapter first introduces these transactions and then gives you the opportunity to become acquainted with the workflow development process using the standard functions. We will pay particular attention to events and where-used lists.

3.1 Relevant Transactions

As an ABAP developer, you are already familiar with Transaction SE80 and the debugging and tracing options you can easily access from there. However, the workflow development involves a wealth of additional transactions. We recommend continuing to use Transaction SE80 (Object Navigator), if possible, and open Transaction SWUD (Workflow Diagnosis) only in a second session. You can navigate to all other relevant transactions from there. For example, you can also access Transactions PFTC (Maintenance: Workflow Tasks) and PFAC (Maintenance: Workflow Rules) via Transaction SE80 by right-clicking on a package and then selecting CREATE • BUSINESS ENGINEERING.

Transaction SWUD, in turn, enables you to navigate to some advanced test transactions for workflow objects that have not been integrated with Transaction SE80.

Memory Aid: Transactions in the Workflow Environment

You should know the following advanced test transactions:

- SE80: Business Engineering Area in the Context of a Development Package
- SWUD: Thematic Test Environment
- SWDM/SWI11: Where-Used List for Tasks and Objects in Workflow Templates

- SWO1: Access to the Business Object Repository (BOR)
  Also: SE80, right-clicking on a package, CREATE • BUSINESS ENGINEERING • BUSINESS OBJECT TYPE
- PFTC: Access to All Workflow Objects Except for Agent Determination Rules
  Also: SE80, right-clicking on a package, CREATE • BUSINESS ENGINEERING • WORKFLOW TEMPLATE/WORKFLOW STANDARD TASK
- PFAC: Access to Agent Determination Rules
  Also: SE80, right-clicking on a package, CREATE • BUSINESS ENGINEERING • WORKFLOW RULE
- SWUS: Start Workflow Templates and Standard Tasks
- SWU0: Simulate Events
- SWUE: Trigger Events
- SWEL/SWELS: Event Trace
- SWEQADM/SWEQBROWSER: Event Queue
- SWU4: Syntax Check for Standard Tasks of a Package
- SWU7: Syntax Check for Workflow Templates of a Package
- SWF_TRC: Workflow Trace (previously SWU8, SWU9, SWU10)
- SWF_GMP: Administrative Overview for Workflow
- SWU3: General Workflow Customizing
- SWE5: Consistency Check for Event Linkage
- SWB_COND: Display Start Conditions

3.2 Workflow Development Process with Standard SAP Functions

In only a few steps, this section introduces a typical development cycle. Let's assume the following scenario: You have been requested to model or modify a workflow that is supposed to control recurring SAP activities. Usually, a workflow starts with an event that you have to identify first. That means you have to provide support to the user department and write a brief transaction script (screenplay protocol) to reflect the most critical cases that are modeled in the workflow.

1. Start the event trace in Transaction SWELS.
2. Together with the user department, go through the core functions of the business process that the new workflow is supposed to map.

3. Make notes of all users involved and all application components of the related transactions.
4. Use Transaction SWEL to analyze the events that were generated during the test run and make notes of the objects involved.
5. Stop the event trace (Transaction SWELS).
6. Use Transaction SWETYPV to check if workflow templates are already linked to the determined results.
7. Analyze the workflow start conditions of the listed objects using Transaction SWB_COND.
8. With Transaction SWDM, search for existing workflow templates for the application components of the workflow objects involved. Also use the structure search in Transaction PFTC.
9. Check the determined workflow templates and standard tasks for reusability via Transactions SWO1 and SWUD.

If events for the exact definition of the appropriate times in the business process are missing, try to generate workflow events with other system triggers.

Possible Trigger Times for Workflow Events

Examples of system triggers include:

- General System Messages (Transaction SWUY)
- Change Documents to Database Tables (Transactions SWU_EWCD, SWEC, SCDO)
- Message Control (Transaction NACE)

Finally, generate copies of all SAP users or groups involved, and model an appropriate organizational structure (Transactions PPOCW, PPOMW).

3.3 Events

Events play a major role in the control of the Workflow Engine. The mechanism for the generation and delivery of events is used for various purposes. We can thus assume that you work with events on a daily basis and have to become acquainted with the exact route an event takes in the system.

To ensure "sound" conditions in your development system, execute Transaction SWE5 (Consistency Check for Event Linkages) together with the SAP Basis team and eliminate all possible error situations. You may have to delete unnecessary event linkages.

The following sections briefly discuss the difference between event type linkage and event instance linkage.

3.3.1 Event Type Linkage

Event type linkages are supposed to *always* trigger a response from the Workflow Engine without considering the exact key value of the object that is linked to the event.

You can use Transaction SWETYPV (also SWE2) to manage this linkage category. The section on check function modules in Chapter 4 further discusses the options for influencing the event delivery via programming.

First, you only link workflow templates with a workflow-relevant event in Transaction SWE2 (see Figure 3.1).

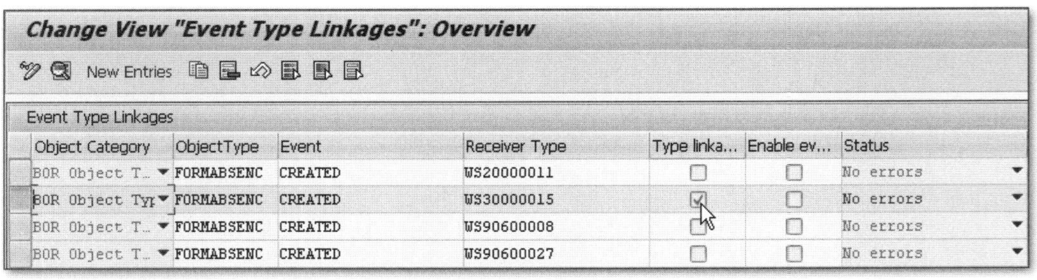

Figure 3.1 Transaction SWETYPV—Active Event Linkage to a Workflow Template

Transaction SWU0 enables you to verify if an event type linkage functions properly. Here, you simulate the delivery of an event, and you can determine which workflow templates would be started if the system generated the respective event.

Figure 3.2 shows the result of an event simulation for the `CREATED` event for the `FORMABSENC` BOR object.

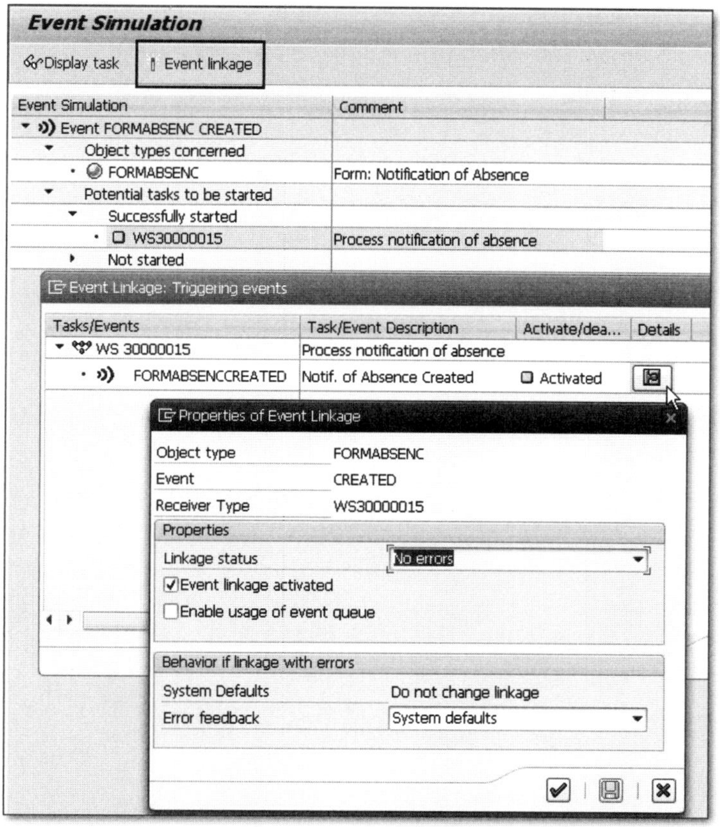

Figure 3.2 Transaction SWU0—Simulation of the Event "FORMABSENC.CREATED"

If you've selected a task in the simulation event, the EVENT LINKAGE button takes you to a dialog that provides the DETAILS icon () for some events. This way you can also modify the event type linkage.

3.3.2 Event Instance Linkage

Event instance linkages are supposed to trigger a response from the Workflow Engine *only* if the event refers to a specific key value of a workflow object; that is, a clearly identified instance. This linkage category is used, for example, if a workflow has already started and individual steps within this workflow template are waiting for a terminating event.

These linkages are not maintained explicitly. Instead, the system enters the instance linkage at the runtime of a workflow. When an event that refers to a specific instance of a workflow object is received, the event linkage is executed and deleted from the list of instance linkages.

3.4 Where-Used Lists in SAP Business Workflow

Experience has shown that ABAP programmers search for a bottom-up where-used list for ABAP functions when they start the workflow programming. In other words, they know an ABAP Objects class or a BOR object and search for all workflow steps that use it. This method is currently not integrated very elegantly into the development environment.

However, there is a useful transaction called SWDM (Business Workflow Explorer), which is unfortunately often overlooked as the term *where-used list* is not explicitly mentioned.

The following scenarios show you how to reach a where-used list.

3.4.1 From Object to Standard Task to Workflow Template

In Transaction SWDM, start a new request by clicking the Select Search Area button ( ). On the Object tab of the next dialog, enter the workflow objects that are supposed to be considered in the search for workflow standard tasks.

In the next detail view, select one of the determined standard tasks on the right-hand side of the screens. Click the Where-Used List icon ( ), and then navigate to a list of workflows that use this standard task (see Figure 3.3).

Due to its options for navigating to workflow development transactions, Transaction SWDM is a good starting point for workflow development. If your new workflow is based on existing tasks, you can quickly generate a copy of an existing workflow and use it as a working basis.

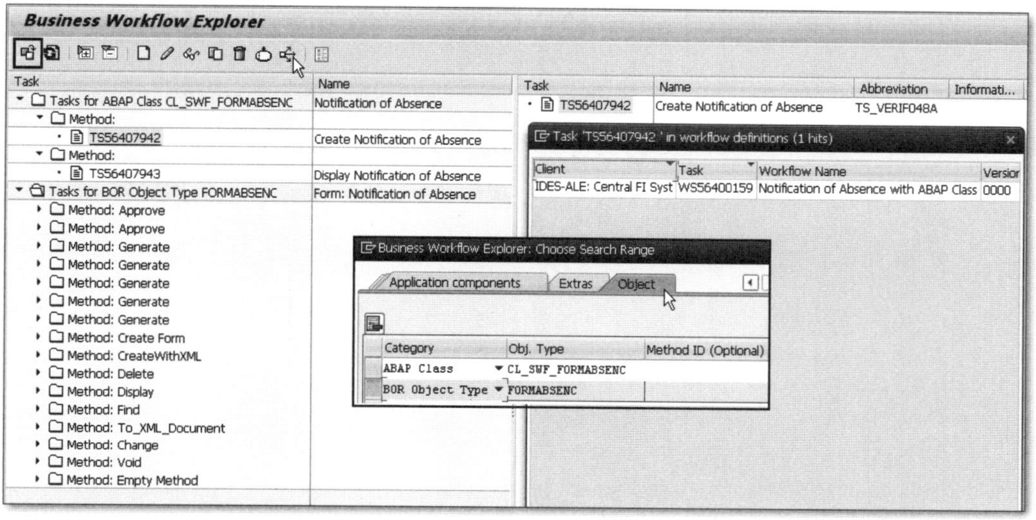

Figure 3.3 Transaction SWDM—Where-Used List for Workflow Objects

3.4.2 From BOR Object to Standard Task (Classic)

To find the standard tasks that use a specific BOR object, navigate to Transaction SWO1 (Business Object Builder), select the BOR object, and follow the menu path Utilities • Where-Used List • Used in Tasks (see Figure 3.4).

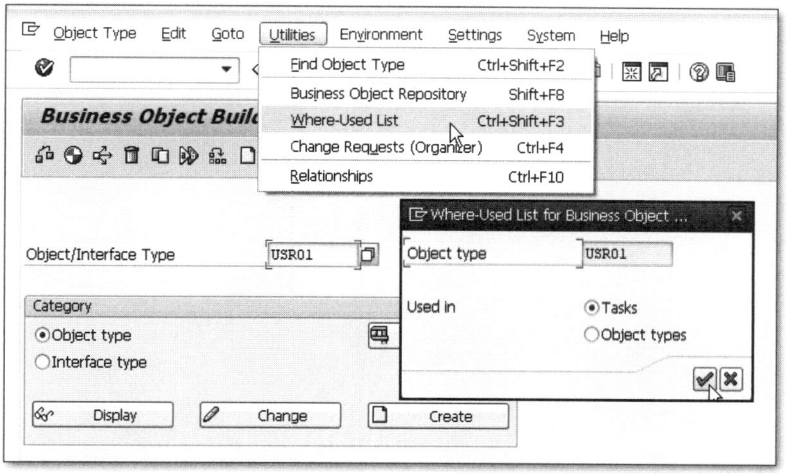

Figure 3.4 Where-Used List for BOR Objects in Workflow Tasks

The results list contains both standard tasks (prefix TS) and workflow templates (prefix WS).

3.4.3 From ABAP Objects Class to Standard Task (Classic)

Finding an ABAP Objects class in a standard task is not that easy.

1. First, ensure that the relevant ABAP Objects class implements the IF_WORKFLOW interface (see Figure 3.5).

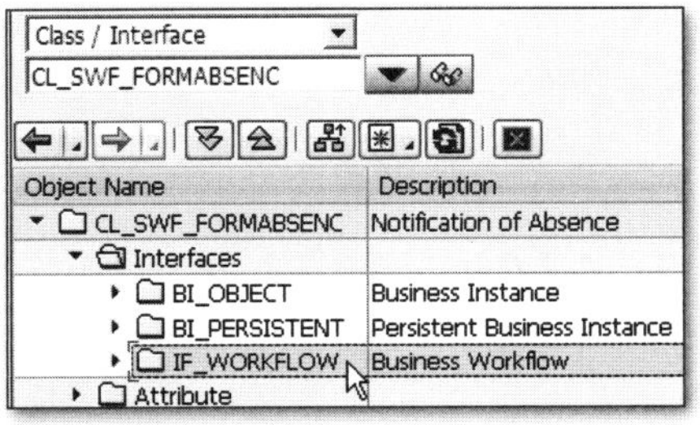

Figure 3.5 ABAP Objects Class with Workflow Interface

2. Then, in Transaction SE37, call the RH_TASKS_OF_WF_OBJECT_TYPE_GET function module with the name of the searched-for ABAP Objects class in the ACT_CLSNAM parameter and CL constant in the ACT_METHTYPE parameter (see Figure 3.6).

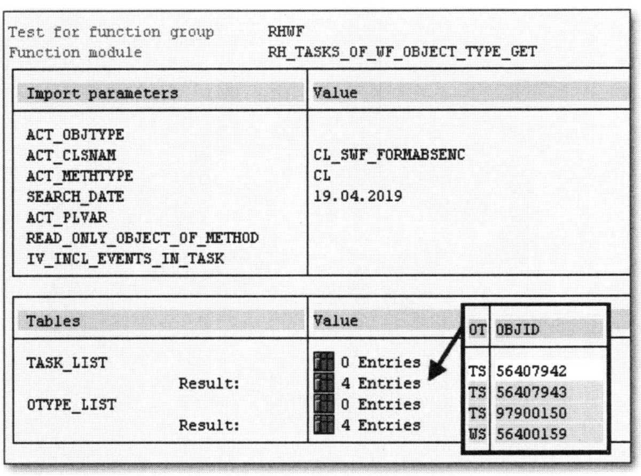

Figure 3.6 Where-Used List for ABAP Objects Classes in Tasks

Table TASK_LIST now contains the list of workflow tasks and templates.

3.4.4 From Standard Task to Workflow Template

Transaction SWI11 (Where-Used List for Tasks) helps you find the correct step that uses a specific workflow task in a workflow template.

The Display Step icon () navigates you to the selected workflow template in the quick view of the Workflow Builder (see Figure 3.7).

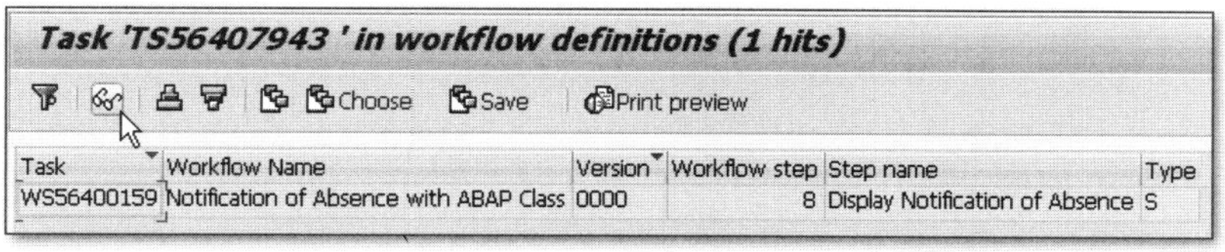

Figure 3.7 Transaction SWI11—Where-Used List of Tasks in Templates

Please note that Transaction SWI11 also enables you to find standard tasks (TS) and subworkflows (WS). This closes the circle from ABAP functions to workflow templates.

4 Methods, Work Items, and Events

Work items are delivered to users or executed in the background. The functions that are supposed to be executed are included in methods. Any systematic impacts or changes in the SAP system may be signaled to the Workflow using events. This chapter explains the concepts behind these terms in detail.

Technically, each step in a workflow template is a work item. Work items, in turn, refer to methods that are supposed to be executed. And the lifecycle of a work item is often controlled by events.

4.1 Types of Methods in the Workflow

Workflow terminology differentiates between synchronous and asynchronous *methods*. These methods include the actual ABAP functions and can be provided via BOR objects or ABAP Objects classes. Methods are integrated with standard tasks and then used in *dialog steps* and *background steps* or called as *secondary methods*.

Synchronous methods allow for directly returning export parameters to the calling program, and this program can then evaluate the triggered exceptions.

Synchronous methods communicate directly with the calling program. Ideally, parameters, events, and exceptions are available after a short wait time. Regarding content, the most important export parameter should be defined as a result parameter (`RESULT` container element). If this result parameter refers to a DDIC domain with defined values, this method provides good support for the modeling of workflows. The workflow designer then allows for automatic navigation using the result parameter.

Asynchronous methods cannot return export parameters, because the responsibility for executing the actual program was handed over to an update task. If the calling program of an asynchronous method receives an exception, it receives the exception merely from the synchronous part that tries to configure the update task. Asynchronous methods must receive their results via result parameters from a workflow event.

In real life, asynchronous methods are to be expected more frequently than you might think. For example, if the user navigates to one of the modern, more complex transactions (such as MIRO), you usually cannot determine if the user actually finished his work simply because he exited the transaction. You therefore often have to respond to BOR events that are generated by this transaction. Only after they have been received can you continue with the workflow processing.

While waiting for a terminating event, the calling program of an asynchronous method cannot assume that the container elements in the workflow contain correct values. After the event and the corresponding binding have been received, you should use the SWC_REFRESH_OBJECT macro to force the new formatting of attributes and container content.

Dialog steps are methods that require a user action. It doesn't matter if they were modeled synchronously or asynchronously. If the method triggers exceptions, you have to model a follow-up step for this exception in the workflow. If you don't do this, the work item remains in the SAP Business Workplace of the processing agent in case of temporary errors. System errors set the workflow to the ERROR status.

Background steps are methods that don't require user action, which means they also don't require agent determination. The user who executes background steps is always the internal system user of the Workflow Engine (WF-BATCH). Again, it doesn't matter if the underlying methods were modeled synchronously or asynchronously. If the method triggers exceptions, you have to model a follow-up step for this exception in the workflow. If you don't do this, the system attempts a new execution after some wait time in case of temporary errors. This can be avoided by using a repeat counter.

If you model a repeat counter, the step is repeated accordingly. Only afterward does the system set the step to the ERROR status or continue with a modeled follow-up step. This procedure is implemented by the SWWERRE background job.

While a method is processed within the workflow template, it is monitored by the *work item manager*. Deadline monitoring implemented by the SWWDHEX background job is also active. You can even define a condition for creating or not creating a work item. This can be done in the Workflow Builder in the details of a workflow method on the CONDITIONS tab. Figure 4.1 shows this in a sample workflow (here, WF_VERIFY030 workflow template).

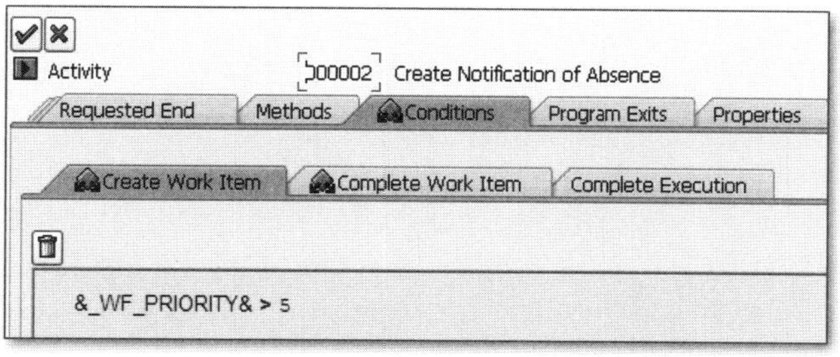

Figure 4.1 Conditions for the Work Item

The work item manager also ensures that *before methods* and *after methods* are executed before a method in a standard task is executed. In parallel to the execution of the *main method*, the system starts all defined *secondary methods*.

A simple example of a secondary method is the simultaneous display of an image from the archive when invoices or goods receipts are processed by the main method. Along with the actual transaction, the archive document is displayed in an additional mode.

Memory Aid: Main and Secondary Methods

If several before, secondary, or after methods are defined, they are started in random order.

According to SAP Note 1334035 (Problems when Executing Secondary Methods), main and secondary methods should always have the same object category. That means you should use either only BOR methods or ABAP Objects methods for each step. A combination of both categories is not fully supported.

Figure 4.2 shows a step with a secondary method in the demonstration workflow WF_Verify026.

The definition of these additional methods can vary in each step of a workflow template. That is why access is provided via the details of a step in the Workflow Builder.

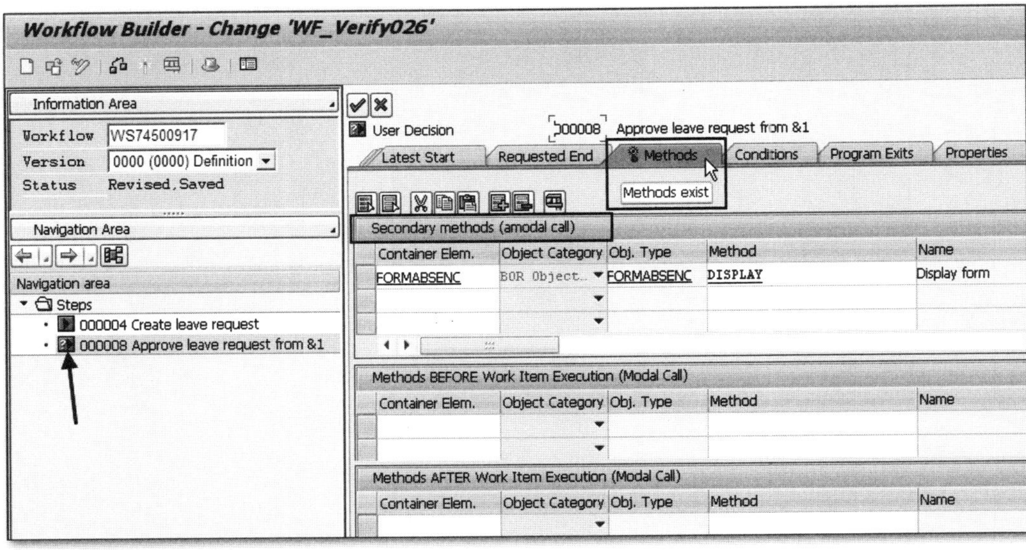

Figure 4.2 Secondary, Before, and After Methods

4.2 Types and Statuses of Work Items

Table 4.1 shows the following most important types of work items:

- *Background work items* are automatically executed and are not displayed in the SAP Business Workplace.
- A *missed deadline work item* is generated when a defined deadline has been missed.
- A *wait step work item* indicates that the system waits for the receipt of events. Both internal and cross-system events can be delivered as wait step work items.
- A *workflow work item* represents a (sub)workflow that is supposed to be processed.
- A *dialog work item* is a workflow step that is supposed to be executed by a user.

The abbreviations shown in Table 4.1 enable you to select these work items; for example, in Transaction SWI1. Table 4.1 shows the most important work item types.

Work Item Type	Abbreviation
Background work item	B
Missed deadline work item	D
Wait step work item	E
(Sub)workflow work item	F
Dialog work item	W

Table 4.1 Most Important Work Item Types

Table 4.2 shows the most important work item statuses.

Status Name	Meaning
WAITING	Waiting
READY	Ready
SELECTED	Selected
STARTED	In process
ERROR	Erroneous
COMPLETED	Completed
CANCELLED	Logically deleted

Table 4.2 Most Important Work Item Statuses

Let's take a closer look at the statuses:

- **WAITING and READY**
  The history of a work items usually starts with WAITING if the preferred start date hasn't been reached yet or with READY if it has been delivered in the SAP Business Workplace.

  You can extensively manipulate work items that have the READY status using the Workflow API (WAPI). The asynchronous procedure for retroactively defining the responsible agent with an ABAP Objects method is based on this API.

- **SELECTED**
  When a user reserves the work item, it changes to the SELECTED status and is no longer displayed in the SAP Business Workplace of other agents.

- **STARTED**
  While the main method of the workflow step is processed, the work item has the STARTED status.
- **ERROR**
  If exceptions occur whose handling has not been modeled, the work item is set to the ERROR status. With a successful result, the work item changes to the COMPLETED status.
- **CANCELLED and COMPLETED**
  The logical deletion (CANCELLED) is an option for canceling the processing. CANCELLED or COMPLETED are thus the typical final statuses in the lifecycle of a work item.

"SAP_WAPI" Interface

There is a very powerful API for the manipulation of work items at runtime that can be used in the Workflow Engine and its components. However, it would go beyond the scope of this book to provide detailed information. You should concern yourself with the SWRC, SWRI, and SWRR function groups and with the `CL_SWF_RUN_WIM_FACTORY` class.

SAP has guaranteed the long-term provision of `SAP_WAPI`. Many of the modules are RFC-enabled but can also be used to control the Workflow Engine remotely and play a major role in the communication between the Java stack and ABAP stack regarding the Web Dynpro topic. Table 4.3 shows the most important modules and is intended as a motivation for looking more closely at this topic.

SWRI Function Group	
Function Module	**Meaning**
`SAP_WAPI_WORKITEMS_BY_DEADLINE`	Work items by missed deadline
`SAP_WAPI_WORKITEMS_BY_ERROR`	Work items with ERROR status
`SAP_WAPI_WORKITEMS_BY_FREQUENC`	Work items by frequency
`SAP_WAPI_WORKITEMS_BY_TASK`	Work items by tasks
`SAP_WAPI_WORKITEMS_TO_OBJECT`	Work items for object
`SAP_WAPI_OBJECTS_IN_WORKITEM`	Objects in a work item
`SAP_WAPI_GET_DEPENDENT_WIS`	Read dependent work items

Table 4.3 Critical "SAP_WAPI" Function Modules

SWRC Function Group	
Function Module	**Meaning**
SAP_WAPI_COUNT_WORKITEMS	Number of work items for a user
SAP_WAPI_EXECUTE_WORKITEM	Execute work item
SAP_WAPI_FORWARD_WORKITEM	Forward work item
SAP_WAPI_PUT_BACK_WORKITEM	Put work item back
SAP_WAPI_REJECT_WORKITEM	Reject work item
SAP_WAPI_RESERVE_WORKITEM	Select work item
SAP_WAPI_RESUBMIT_WORKITEM	Resubmit work item
SAP_WAPI_GET_WORKITEM_DETAIL	Read details of work item
SWRR	
Function Module	**Meaning**
SAP_WAPI_CREATE_EVENT	Generate event
SAP_WAPI_ASYNC_RULE_COMPLETE	Set agent of the asynchronous rule resolution
SAP_WAPI_START_WORKFLOW	Start workflow
SAP_WAPI_WRITE_CONTAINER	Write container
SAP_WAPI_READ_CONTAINER	Read container

Table 4.3 Critical "SAP_WAPI" Function Modules (Cont.)

With this basic collection of function modules, you can substantially manipulate the flow logic of the Workflow Engine.

4.3 Events and Their Delivery

Events are an appropriate and the most frequently used method for starting workflows. The system can generate various events. However, always initiating a workflow template to determine that there is nothing to do in this case in a first step would be a complete waste of resources.

The Workflow Builder therefore enables you to provide conditions for the triggering events of a workflow template.

For this purpose, click the BASIC DATA button (icon) in the Workflow Builder overview and then the VERSION-INDEPENDENT and START EVENTS tabs.

Enable the event linkage and define a binding and a start condition. The start condition could be, for example, that a workflow template is started only if the event contained includes a certain value. Figure 4.3 shows an example of a linkage entry with a condition.

Figure 4.3 Start Events with Binding and Condition

After you save this entry in the Workflow Builder, Transaction SWETYPV contains a corresponding line (see Figure 4.4).

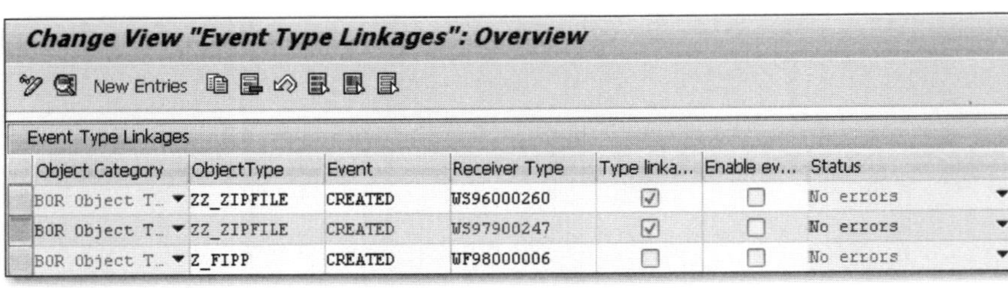

Figure 4.4 Active Event Linkage in Transaction SWETYPV

Double-clicking this line takes you to the details of the event type linkage. Owing to Customizing in the Workflow Builder (see Figure 4.5), a RECEIVER FUNCTION MODULE and a CHECK FUNCTION MODULE were entered in the event type linkage.

The RECEIVER FUNCTION MODULE is the part of ABAP code that starts the content of the event container; that is, a workflow template. The SWW_WI_CREATE_VIA_EVENT_IBF module shown in the figure is very useful for in-depth studies. It uses many of the container-relevant interfaces that are introduced in this book.

You can also define an ABAP Objects method as the receiver. One example of this option is the CL_SWF_EVT_TOOL_EVENT_MAIL class, which implements the BI_EVENT_HANDLER_STATIC interface. The requested method, ON_EVENT, can be used as the receiver in the event type linkage.

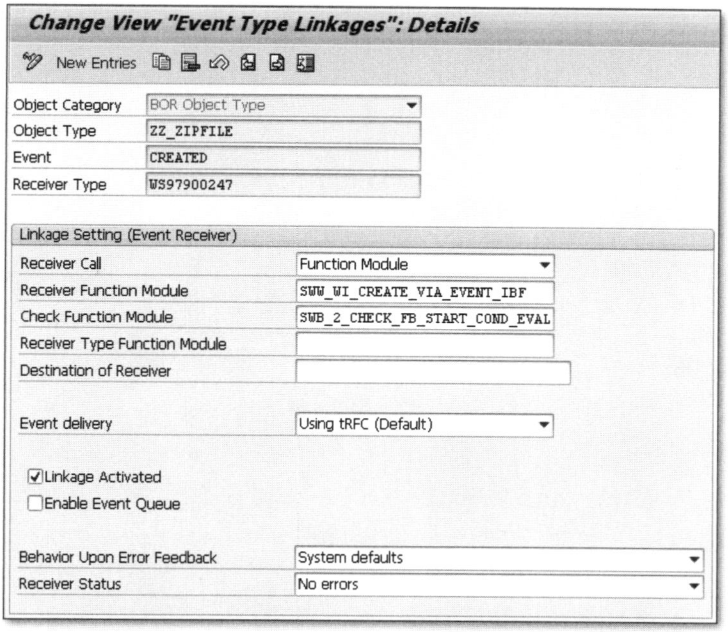

Figure 4.5 Generated Entry with Receiver and Check Function Module

4.3.1 Check and Receiver Type Function Modules

Based on the event container and system situation, check function modules, such as the SWB_2_CHECK_FB_START_COND_EVAL module (which is automatically entered here), are supposed to check whether it makes sense to enable the workflow template. The rule is simple: If the function module doesn't generate an exception, the system can start the workflow template.

Listing 4.1 shows a very simple `CHECK` function module that generates an exception if the event is not supposed to be delivered to this receiver.

```
FUNCTION CHECK_OBJECT_TYPE_IDOCAPPL.
*"----------------------------------------------
*" IMPORTING
*"    VALUE(EVENT) LIKE  SWETYPECOU-EVENT
*"    VALUE(RECTYPE) LIKE  SWETYPECOU-RECTYPE
*"    VALUE(OBJTYPE) LIKE  SWETYPECOU-OBJTYPE
*"    VALUE(OBJKEY) LIKE  SWEINSTCOU-OBJKEY
*"  TABLES
*"    EVENT_CONTAINER STRUCTURE  SWCONT
*"  EXCEPTIONS
*"    CHECK_FAILED
*"----------------------------------------------

  CONSTANTS:
    C_OBJTYPE_IDOCAPPL LIKE
              SWETYPECOU-OBJTYPE VALUE 'IDOCAPPL',
    C_EVT_OBJTYPE       LIKE
              SWCONT-ELEMENT VALUE '_EVT_OBJTYPE'.

  DATA: INITIATING_OBJTYPE LIKE
              SWETYPECOU-OBJTYPE.

  SWC_GET_ELEMENT EVENT_CONTAINER
              C_EVT_OBJTYPE INITIATING_OBJTYPE.

  IF INITIATING_OBJTYPE <> C_OBJTYPE_IDOCAPPL.
    RAISE CHECK_FAILED.
  ENDIF.

ENDFUNCTION.
```

Listing 4.1 Simple Check Function Module

On the basis of the event container, the receiver type function module is responsible for returning an appropriate workflow template that is supposed to process the event.

The Customizing entry (if available) from Transaction SWETYPV is transferred as a proposal in the `generic_rectype` parameter.

Listing 4.2 shows a possible receiver type function module.

```
FUNCTION CVWF_EVENT_REC_DOKST_GET.
*"-------------------------------------------------
*" IMPORTING
*"    OBJTYPE          LIKE  SWETYPECOU-OBJTYPE
*"    OBJKEY           LIKE  SWEINSTCOU-OBJKEY
*"    EVENT            LIKE  SWEINSTCOU-EVENT
*"    GENERIC_RECTYPE LIKE  SWETYPECOU-RECTYPE
*" EXPORTING
*"    RECTYPE          LIKE  SWETYPECOU-RECTYPE
*" TABLES
*"    EVENT_CONTAINER STRUCTURE  SWCONT
*" EXCEPTIONS
*"    NO_RECTYPE
*"-------------------------------------------------
  INCLUDE <CNTN01>.

  DATA : L_DOKST LIKE DRAW-DOKST.
  DATA : BEGIN OF DRAWKEY,
           DOKAR LIKE DRAW-DOKAR,
           DOKNR LIKE DRAW-DOKNR,
           DOKVR LIKE DRAW-DOKVR,
           DOKTL LIKE DRAW-DOKTL,
         END OF DRAWKEY.

  SWC_GET_ELEMENT EVENT_CONTAINER
             'DOCUMENTSTATUS' L_DOKST.

  DRAWKEY = OBJKEY.

  SELECT SINGLE * FROM  TDWS
         WHERE  DOKAR       = DRAWKEY-DOKAR
         AND    DOKST       = L_DOKST.

  RECTYPE = TDWS-OTYPE.
  RECTYPE+2 = TDWS-OBJID.


ENDFUNCTION.
```

Listing 4.2 Simple Receiver Type Function Module

If you use a receiver type function module, you mustn't enter an event type linkage in the workflow template, because this would bypass the effect of the function module. When you are developing receiver type function modules, note that these are executed in context and with authorizations of the event creator. The ABAP code in receiver type function modules should therefore be as independent of authorizations as possible.

4.3.2 Event Queue

In real-life scenarios, some interfaces often generate numerous events at night, because batch processing is implemented at this time with reduced load.

If each of these events leads to a tRFC call and wants to start a workflow template, this can result in a load-related error scenario. Consequently, you should straighten out the system load with a queue.

In the event type linkage, the ENABLE EVENT QUEUE checkbox (see Figure 4.5) enables you to define whether you want to allow for event delivery in a queue. If this checkbox is selected for a specific event, the event is written to a special queue, and the receiver module is entered as the update task.

You are already familiar with Transactions SWEQADM and SWEQBROWSER. Activate the event queue, and remove any old events that haven't been delivered yet. You also have to schedule the background job for the queue processing. If an error occurs when the event is delivered via the queue, the queue administrator receives an email.

The system uses a standard setting to decide whether the linkage of the event is supposed to be completely deactivated, to be selected as erroneous, or to remain unchanged after an error has occurred. This setting is located on the BASIC DATA tab in Transaction SWEQADM (see Figure 4.6).

Usually, the MARK LINKAGE AS HAVING ERRORS setting for RECEIVER ERROR FEEDBACK is the appropriate choice if there is a queue administrator. With this setting, future events are stored and not processed until the originally affected event has been delivered manually.

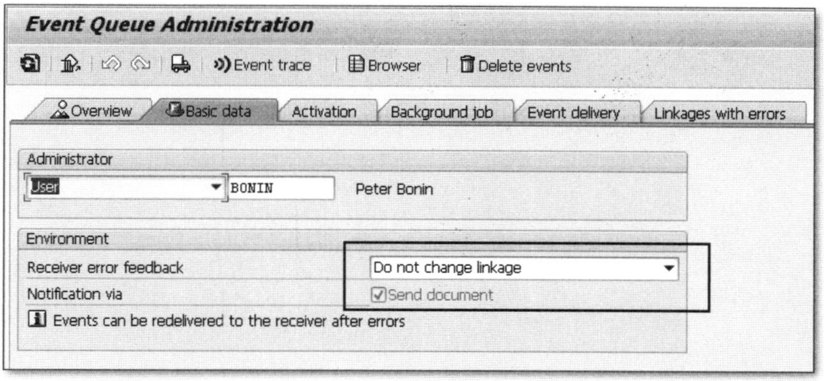

Figure 4.6 Standard Setting for the Event Linkage After Delivery Errors

5 Intervening in the Agent Determination

In the workflow environment, the agent determination controls who is to be involved in the individual workflow steps. Besides the actual functionality, this is the most significant task of a Workflow Engine. This chapter describes the most essential options to intervene in the *agent determination*—the part of the Workflow Engine that determines to whom a work item is sent.

5.1 Creating a Workflow

To obtain a workflow that particularly emphasizes the agent determination, let's use a copy of a workflow template that is used to test the Workflow Engine in Transaction SWUI_VERIFY (Start Test Workflow). The demo workflow `WF_Verify038` has a strikingly simple functionality: It does nothing—at least not in dialog. But because all dialog work items have an agent determination, this example is very well suited to examine this area.

To copy an existing workflow template, proceed as follows:

1. Copy the demo workflow `WF_Verify038` in Transaction PFAC (Maintain Workflow Rule). This workflow creates a dialog work item without functionality that shows an explicit deadlines dialog window. In the initial screen of Transaction PFAC, select WORKFLOW TEMPLATE as the task type and WF_VERIFY038 as the task.
2. Press the [Enter] key. The system takes you to a simplified search help and selects the workflow template based on the search text entered.
3. Copy ( ) the workflow template to one of your ABAP packages and to the Z or Y namespace, if required (see Figure 5.1).
4. Finally, write down the number assigned to your new workflow template `ZWF_Bearb01`.

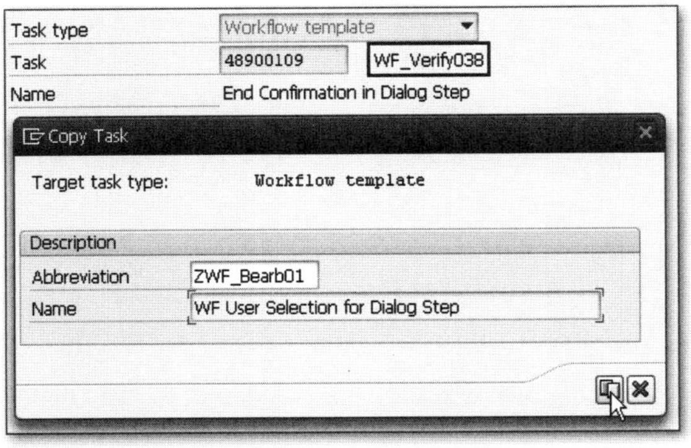

Figure 5.1 Copying the Demo Workflow "WF_Verify_038"

5.2 Determining and Selecting the Agent Determination Dynamically

To obtain a very clear example of the agent determination, you now add a new step to the previously copied workflow. This step offers all possible users for selection.

For this purpose, in Transaction PFTC click the CHANGE icon (✎) for the newly created workflow template and then click the WORKFLOW BUILDER button on the BASIC DATA tab of the overview screen that appears. This takes you to the edit mode of the Workflow Builder. In the graphical workflow editor, double-click the EMPTY DIALOG WITH END CONFIRMATION step (see Figure 5.2).

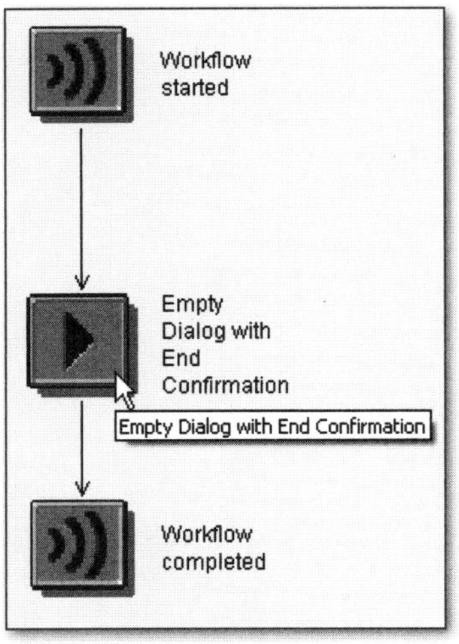

Figure 5.2 Simple Dialog Step—Copy from "WF_Verify038"

You now add another step to this workflow that enables you to determine agents dynamically.

Remove the definition of the responsible agent in the detail view of the EMPTY DIALOG WITH END CONFIRMATION step. No entry should be available under AGENTS in the next step. Delete the &_WF_INITIATOR& entry in the INITIATOR OF WORKFLOW field as illustrated in Figure 5.3 because the dialog step is not supposed to be sent to the person who triggered the workflow, but instead to another user you specify in a selection dialog.

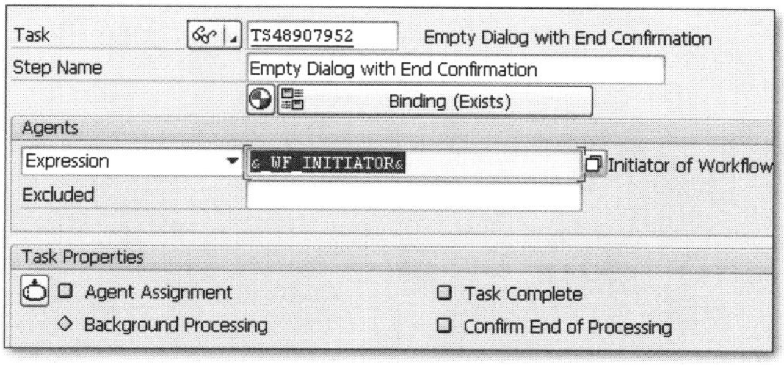

Figure 5.3 Agent Determination Via Expression

Now click the ACCEPT AND BACK icon (✔) to return to the graphical overview of the workflow template, and select the EMPTY DIALOG WITH END CONFIRMATION step again (see ❶ in Figure 5.4).

In the lower-left area of the workflow area, select WORKFLOW WIZARDS ❷ and then select the workflow wizard MODELING SUPPORT • AD HOC: INCLUDE "SELECT EDITOR" (❸).

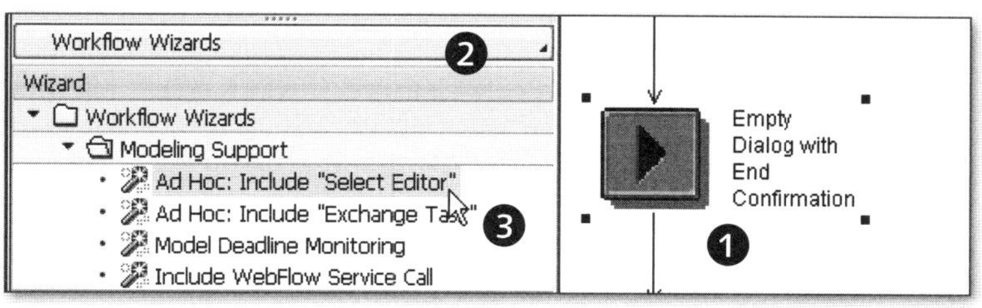

Figure 5.4 Workflow Wizard for Including an Ad Hoc Task

The wizard that appears tells you that you've selected a task with empty agent determination expression and generates another dialog step before this task in the workflow.

This new dialog step is displayed as a dialog window where you are prompted to select one or more agents. Enter a meaningful name for the dialog window in the Title of Selection Dialog Box field, for instance, "Select Agent dynamically," as illustrated in Figure 5.5.

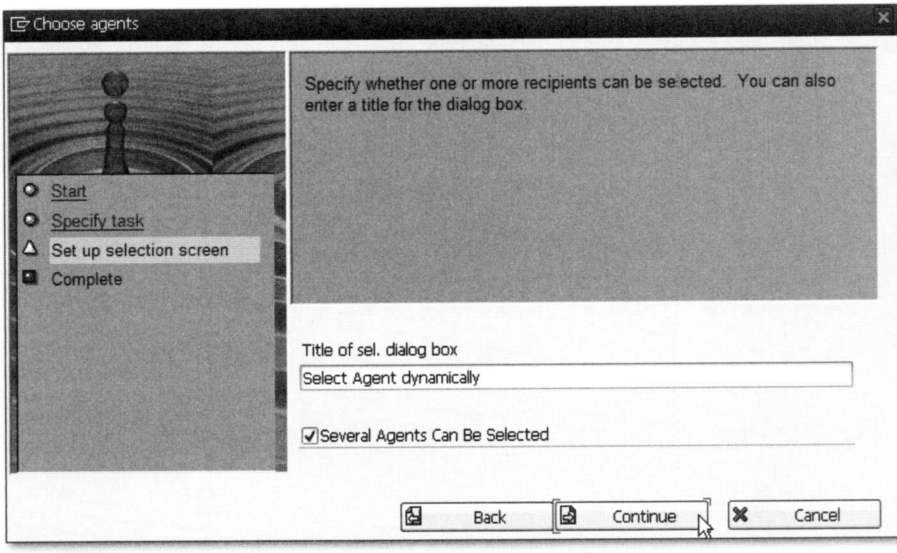

Figure 5.5 Entering the Title for the Selection Dialog

In addition, the wizard creates two elements in the workflow container (see Figure 5.6).

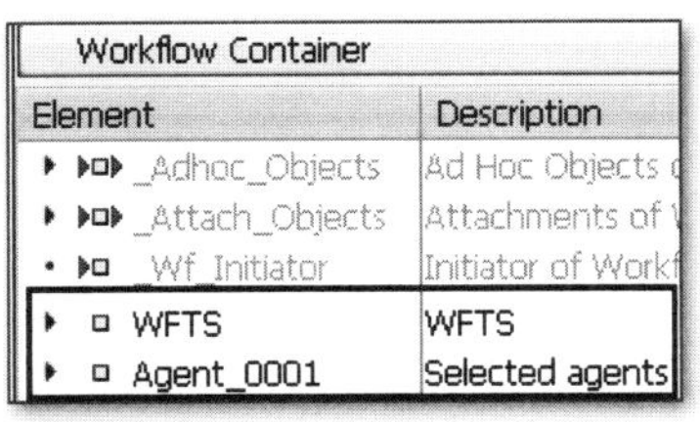

Figure 5.6 Automatically Created Container Elements

The WFTS container element contains a reference to the standard task for which the agent determination is supposed to be performed. The Agent_xxxx container element includes the result of your agent selection in the workflow container. In this case, xxxx is a serial number because this procedure can be used several times in a workflow template. Values can be transported to the following workflow steps via the container elements of the workflow only.

If you now consider the workflow step created by the wizard (see Figure 5.7), you will determine that it also has an expression for the agent determination. This enables you to control which user group A receives a work item to determine an agent from user group B. In this example, the workflow initiator (&_WF_Initiator&) is supposed to run the agent selection.

But first focus on the binding for the task, SELECTION OF AGENTS FOR SUBSEQUENT TASK. Click the BINDING (EXISTS) button (see Figure 5.7).

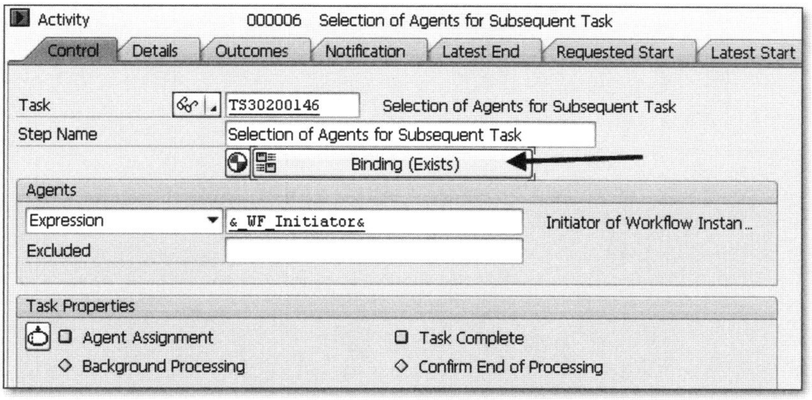

Figure 5.7 Newly Created Step in the Workflow with Binding

The binding provides initial remarks on the function of the generated workflow step. The workflow container forwards some constants to the task container of the standard task, and you receive a list of the agents selected (see &Agent_0001& container element in Figure 5.8).

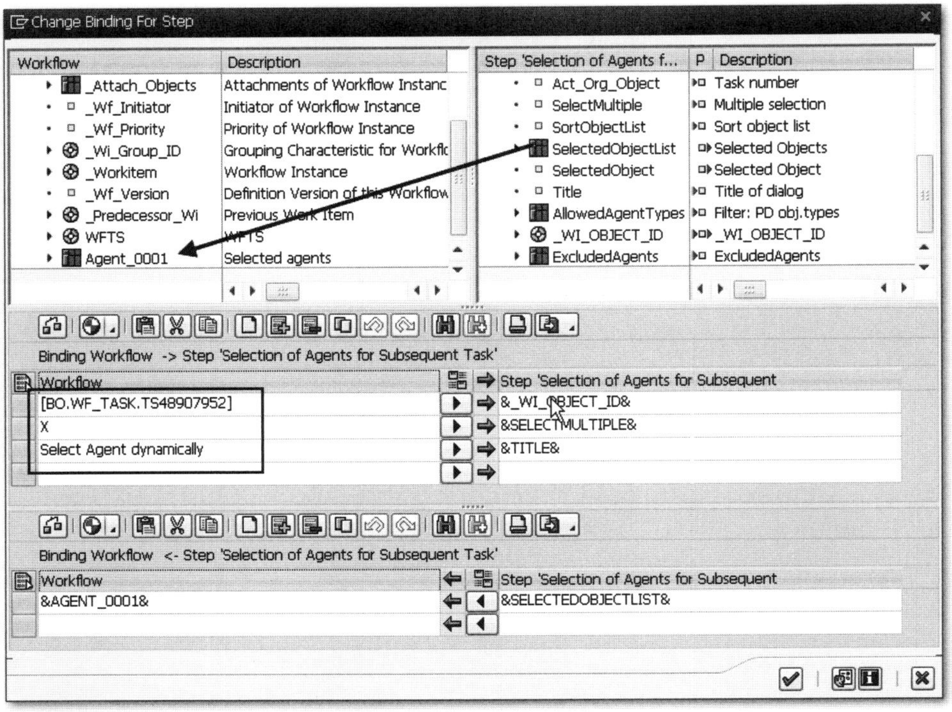

Figure 5.8 Binding for the Dynamic User Selection Step

A noteworthy fact about this binding is that constants are transferred to a standard task.

Exit the detail view of this step by clicking the CONTINUE button (✔), and activate the workflow template by clicking the CREATE AND ACTIVATE RUNTIME VERSION icon ( ).

5.3 Testing the Workflow Template

To test the test environment for the workflow template, click the TEST icon ( ) in the Workflow Builder. The system takes you to the workflow test environment (Transaction SWUS). First, refresh the buffer for the organizational environment so that any changes to the organizational structure of the Workflow Engine are available. Then execute the workflow by clicking the EXECUTE icon ( ) (see Figure 5.9).

Figure 5.9 Refreshing the Buffer for the Organizational Environment

The first workflow step in this test (SELECTION OF AGENTS FOR SUBSEQUENT TASK) now takes you to the selection of users for the second step. Because the subsequent step (EMPTY DIALOG WITH END CONFIRMATION) is a general task, you can send the work item to all organizational units known in the SAP system. The SELECTION dialog window in Figure 5.10 provides help for the selection.

Ensure that as the workflow initiator you are included in the selected set. Use the FIND input field for the ORGANIZATIONAL UNITS to select the organizational units of the demo enterprise you created in Chapter 2 (see Figure 5.10). Confirm your selection (✔ icon).

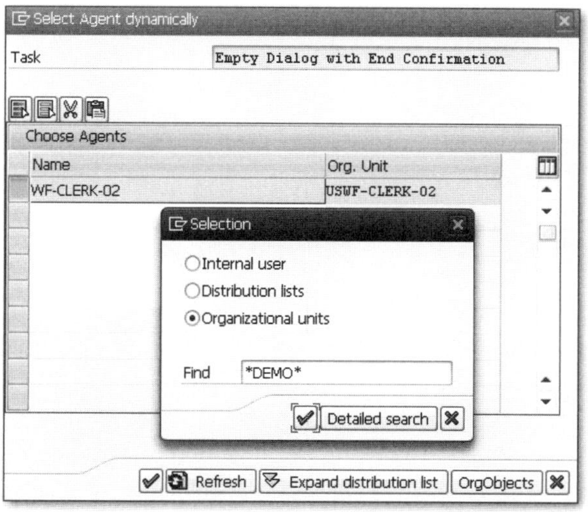

Figure 5.10 Dynamic Agent Determination for General Tasks

Provided that you're included in the set of selected agents, the system displays the dialog window for explicitly completing the work item. Click the AGENTS button as illustrated in Figure 5.11. The message "All users can process this task" indicates that this is a general task. Complete the workflow by clicking the COMPLETE WORK ITEM button.

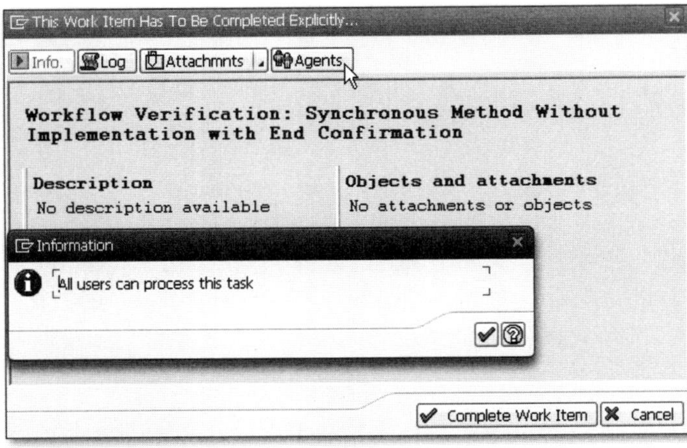

Figure 5.11 Dialog for Explicitly Completing Work Items for a General Task

Once you're back in the test environment for workflows, click the WORKFLOW LOG and LIST WITH TECHNICAL DETAILS icons to navigate to the list with technical details.

In the log, select the step in which you selected the agent(s), and then go to the CONTAINER tab. You should find a list of the selected employees in the lower area of the screen under SELECTEDOBJECTLIST (see Figure 5.12).

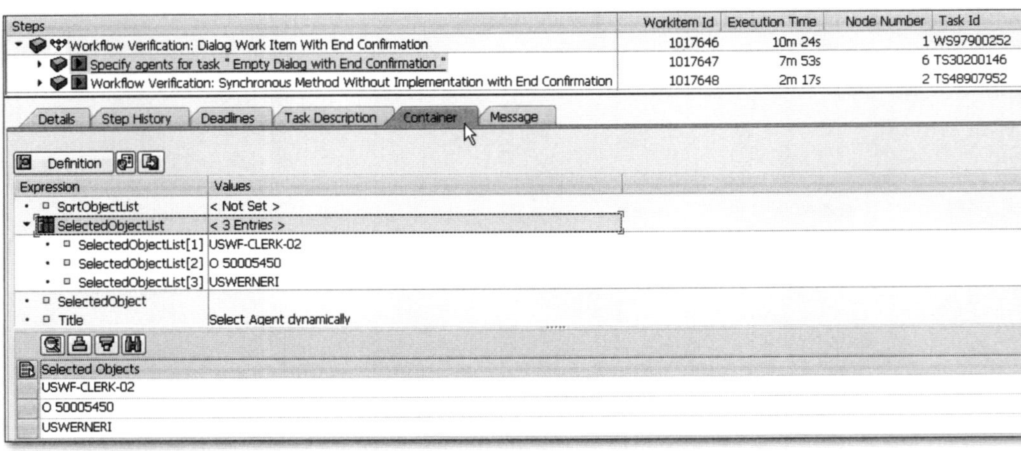

Figure 5.12 Container Contents After Executing First Workflow Step

If you've forgotten to include yourself in the selection of agents, the work item in the inbox of SAP Business Workplace will have been sent to the other selected employees and is now available to them via Transaction SBWP.

To find out which logon ID you must use to further process the workflow, select the last unprocessed step of the workflow in the workflow log with technical details and have the system display a list of selected agents via the context menu under DISPLAY AGENT (see Figure 5.13).

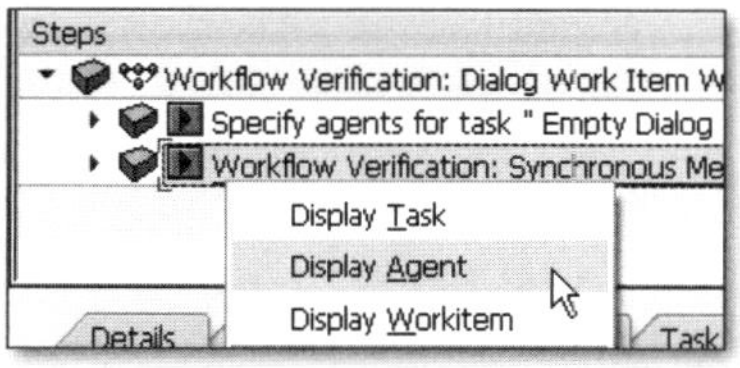

Figure 5.13 "Display Agent" for a Step Still To Be Processed

The goal of this example was to illustrate how you determine the set of responsible agents in the SAP Workflow environment and forward them to standard tasks.

5.4 Modeling the Agent Determination Using Task Groups

In the previous example you determined the agents for a general task. In a real business process, however, it is not desirable to select the "entire enterprise" as possible agents. If, during the development phase, you mainly use dialog steps that are declared as a general task, your workflow may send the work items to all users in the development system. This may cause some confusion. It therefore makes sense to assign the steps in your workflow templates to *task groups*: Some steps in the workflow templates are possibly intended for technical staff, others are for supervisors, and some are supposed to be sent across all departments to all members of the management team.

As the workflow developer, you can now bundle the individual standard tasks of your workflow template by topics in task groups. You can then assign these task groups to a development package to transport them together with the workflow template.

The person to whom you send the workflow template and the task groups doesn't have to maintain the agent assignment for each step but can simplify this work based on your task groups that are presorted by topic. Let's assume that in your workflow, in order to be developed the activities more or less match the departments of your demo enterprise. To do this, proceed as follows:

1. Create three task groups in Transaction PFTC (see Figure 5.14):
   - ZWF_AG_EDV for technical tasks
   - ZWF_AG_FI for commercial tasks
   - ZWF_AG_ALL for general tasks

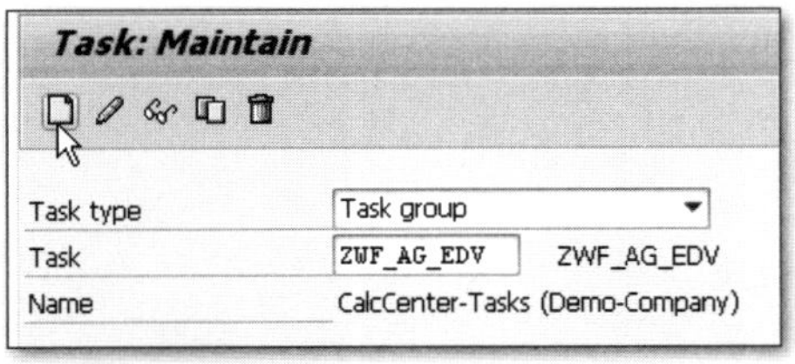

Figure 5.14 Maintaining Task Groups

2. For each of the three task groups, set the RELEASE STATUS to "Released" in the BASIC DATA tab (see Figure 5.15).

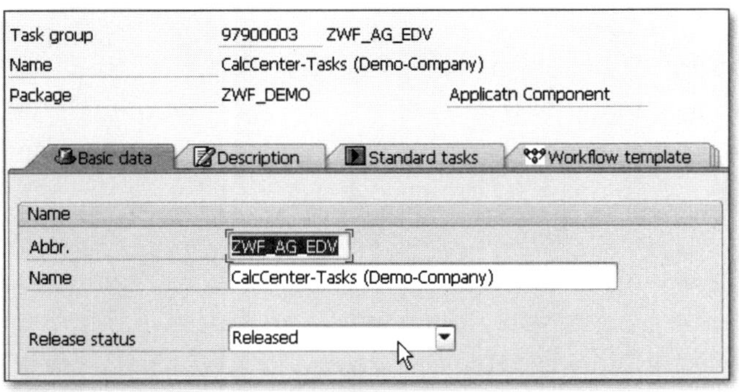

Figure 5.15 Basic Data of a Task Group

3. If the system queries a package assignment when you click SAVE (💾), ensure that the task groups are assigned to the package where you maintain the workflow template.
4. Assign agents to the task groups (in the menu under EXTRAS • AGENT ASSIGNMENT • MAINTAIN).

5. Add the organizational units, which represent the respective department, to the task groups for FI and EDI tasks (see Figure 5.16).

You have now defined the set of possible agents for each task group.

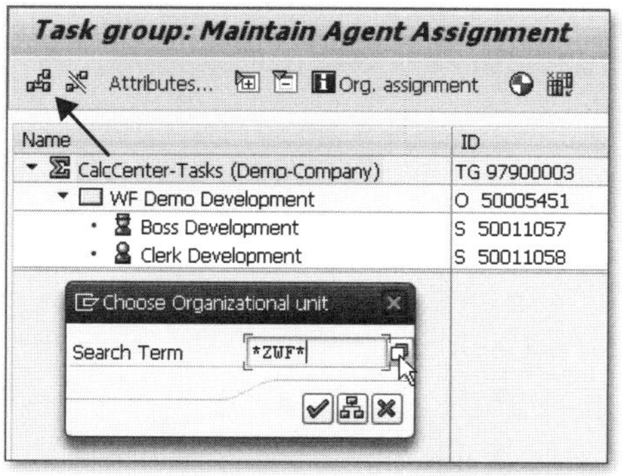

Figure 5.16 Maintaining the Agent Assignment of a Task Group

You also use these task groups for the agent determination in your workflow template. Because the previously used workflow task was declared as a general task and is part of an SAP package, you must first copy this task. To do so, open the workflow template again in Transaction PFTC and go to the Workflow Builder.

Ideally, you will open Transaction PFTC in a second mode because you'll require the maintenance of task groups later on.

1. Open the detail view of the EMPTY DIALOG WITH END CONFIRMATION step by double-clicking the corresponding icon in the workflow template.
2. Select the CONTROL tab. Click the DISPLAY TASK icon ( ) under TASK. The system opens a dropdown list where you select the COPY AND EDIT TASK entry (see Figure 5.17).

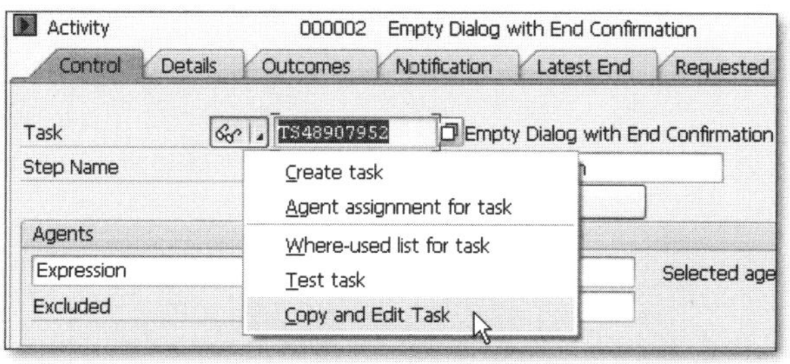

Figure 5.17 Copying a Standard Task in the Workflow Builder

3. Enter a new abbreviation (here "ZWF_Empty") and a name for the new standard task (see Figure 5.18).

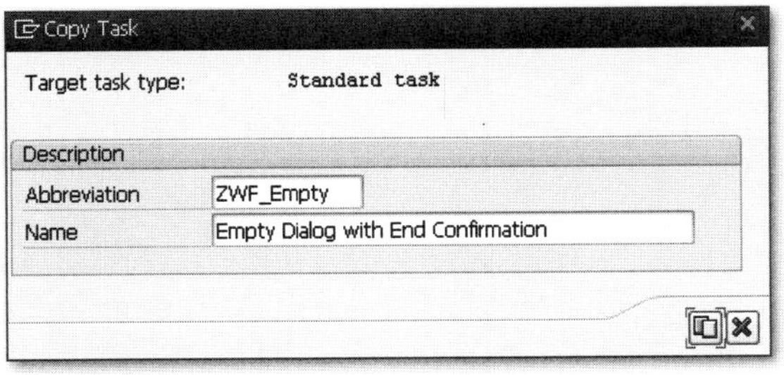

Figure 5.18 Creating a Copy of a Standard Task

4. Change the properties of the agent assignment for this standard task by selecting EXTRAS • AGENT ASSIGNMENT • MAINTAIN from the menu.
5. Then click ATTRIBUTES... and select GENERAL FORWARDING ALLOWED (see Figure 5.19).
6. Accept the changes and return to the standard task overview via the BACK icon (icon).

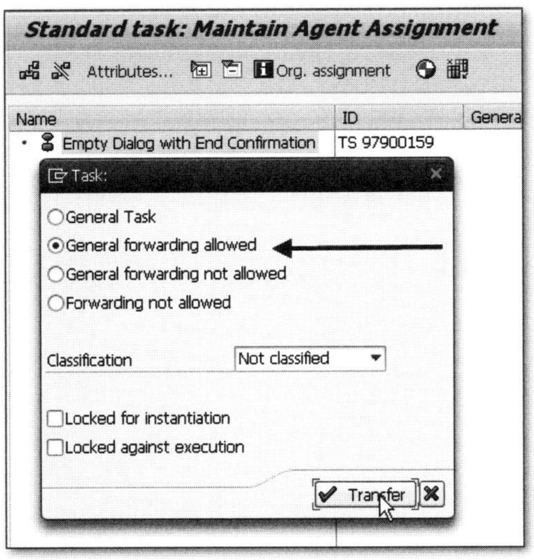

Figure 5.19 Properties of the Agent Assignment

7. Save the newly copied standard task with release status "Released." Write down the name and number assigned to this standard task (see Figure 5.20).

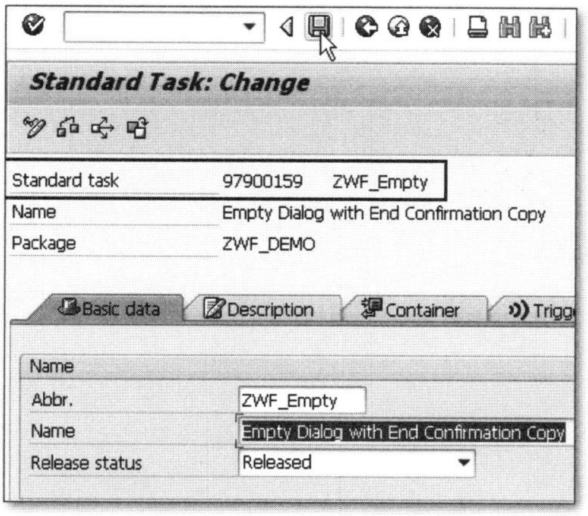

Figure 5.20 Saving a New Standard Task

8. Click the BACK icon (⊛) to return to the Workflow Builder. Check whether the new number of your copy is displayed on the CONTROL tab under TASK.
9. If the system proposes changes to the binding when you accept the copy of the standard task in the workflow step, reject this proposal.
10. Confirm the changes of the workflow step by clicking TRANSFER AND GO TO GRAPHIC (☑).
11. Now go to the detail view of the SELECTION OF AGENTS FOR SUBSEQUENT TASK step.
12. Change the binding by clicking the BINDING (DOES NOT EXIST) button (▤) (see Figure 5.21). Ensure that the number of your new standard task appears in the assignment to the &_WI_OBJECT_ID& container element.
    - By setting S and US in the &ALLOWEDAGENTTYPES& table, you ensure that only positions and SAP users can be selected.
    - By transferring the &_WF_INITIATOR& container element to the &EXCLUDED-AGENTS& table, you prevent the workflow initiator itself from executing the next step. This is frequently required in approval scenarios.

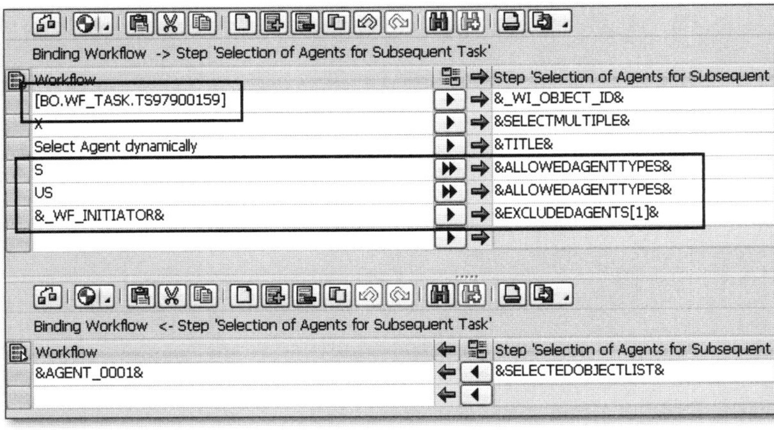

Figure 5.21 New Binding for Dialog Step for Agent Selection

13. Exit the binding editor by clicking the Exit Binding Editor icon (✔).
14. Now exit the detail view of this step clicking the Transfer and Go to Graphic button (✔), and activate the workflow template by clicking the Create and Activate Runtime Version icon ( ).

Before you test the workflow, you must define the new standard task also in the task groups. To do this, proceed as follows:

1. Enter the number of your new standard task on the Standard tasks tab for the task groups ZWF_AG_EDV and ZWF_AG_FI. You can also use the abbreviation (here ZWF_Empty) (see Figure 5.22).

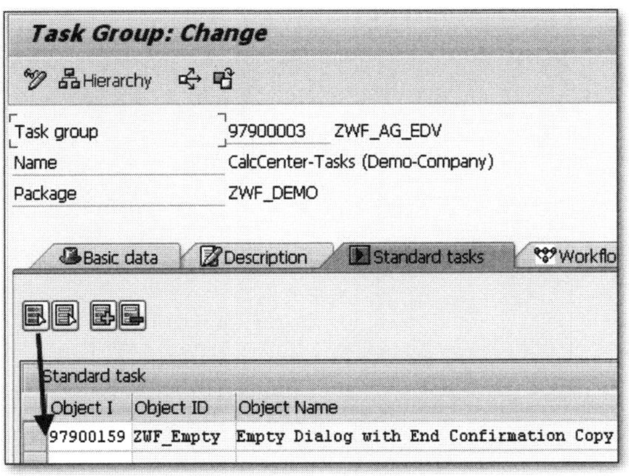

Figure 5.22 Adding a Standard Task to a Task Group

2. Save the task group and exit the maintenance transaction.
3. Now start the workflow template in the test environment by clicking the TEST icon (icon) in the Workflow Builder.

The dialog for the agent selection (dynamic agent determination) now only offers users and organizational units that were determined from the agent assignment in the task groups (see Figure 5.23). The workflow initiator is not provided for selection.

With these changes, you considerably influenced the behavior of the agent determination. The newly created standard task is no longer a general task. As a result, you can no longer select the "entire enterprise" as agents.

The Workflow Engine evaluated the task groups and their agent assignment to determine the set of possible agents, and only those are now available for selection. The workflow initiator was removed from the selection set and is an *excluded agent*. If you want to exit the workflow, you must log on as an SAP user who belongs to the set of possible agents.

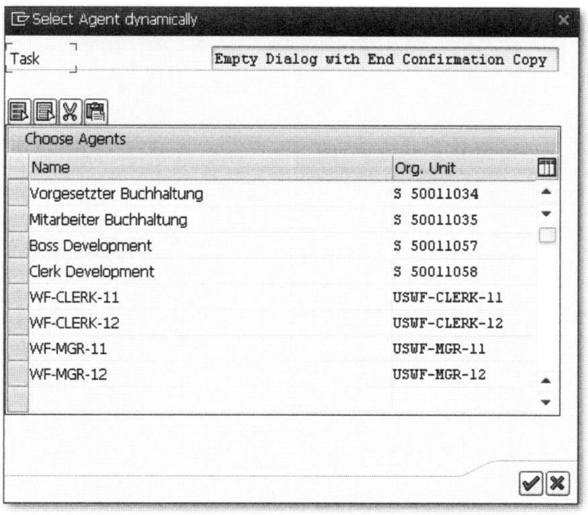

Figure 5.23 Agent Selection for Nongeneral Tasks

5.5 Agent Determination with Responsibilities

Frequently, you may want to define responsibilities for a specific task not via the organizational structure but via concrete value ranges. An often-quoted example refers to a responsibility that depends on the first letter of a customer's or employee's last name. The responsibility can also depend on a numeric value range, for example, an amount. The Workflow Engine comprises a special variant of the agent determination rules for this purpose.

This variant enables you to define and prioritize "from-to" ranges for simple data types. To do this, follow the steps below:

1. Create another copy of the `WF_Verify038` demo workflow in Transaction PFTC (Maintain Workflow Tasks) and name it ZWF_RuleTest.
2. In the Workflow Builder, create a new `RuleVal` data element in the workflow container for this copy (see Figure 5.24).

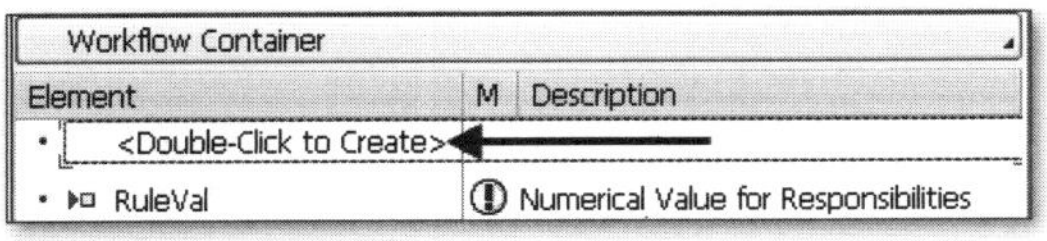

Figure 5.24 Creating a New Container Element Using a Double-Click

3. This container element is supposed to be based on the classic data type NUMC5 (Data Type tab) (❶ in Figure 5.25) and represent a mandatory input element (Mandatory checkbox in the Parameter Settings field group) (❷).

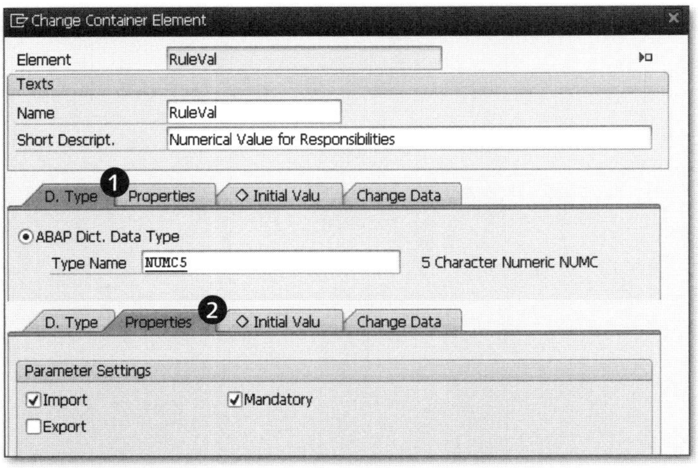

Figure 5.25 New Mandatory Container Element

The system transports a numeric value in the `RuleVal` variable of the workflow container. If you select the MANDATORY checkbox, you must enter a value for the workflow test environment.

4. SAVE (💾) and ACTIVATE ( ) the workflow template.

5.5.1 Creating Rules Based on Responsibilities

Depending on the `RuleVal` variable, which you placed in the workflow container in the previous section, you now need to control the responsibilities for a standard task.

Create a new rule in Transaction PFAC (Maintain Workflow Rule). Specify an abbreviation (here "ZWF_TestVal").

1. On the RULE DEFINITION tab, select "Agent Determination: Responsibilities" in the CATEGORY field. Select the CONSIDER SECONDARY PRIORITIES and TERMINATE IF RULE RESOLUTION WITHOUT RESULT checkboxes (see Figure 5.26).

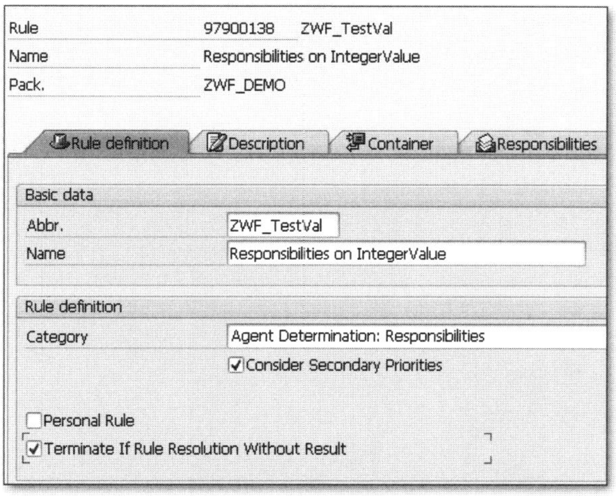

Figure 5.26 Agent Determination Rule by Responsibilities

2. On the CONTAINER tab, click the CREATE ELEMENT ICON (🗋) to create the `RuleVal` data element in the container of the rule exactly as you did in the workflow template; in other words, as a mandatory import element based on NUMC5 (see Figure 5.25).

   The rule container view now looks like what is shown in Figure 5.24.

3. Now go to the RESPONSIBILITIES tab and click the CREATE RESPONSIBILITY ICON () to create a new responsibility including an abbreviation and a validity period (see Figure 5.27).

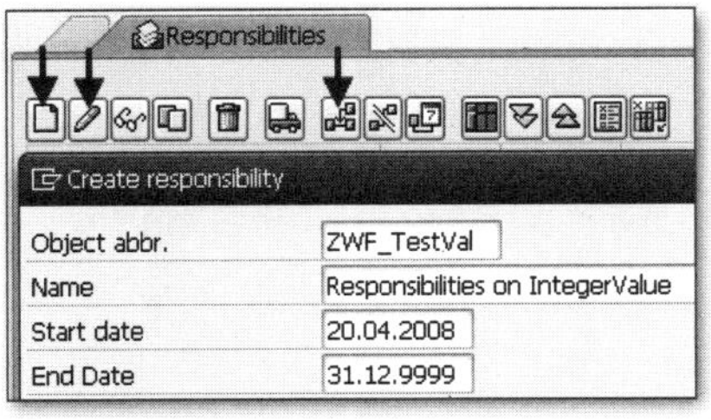

Figure 5.27 Creating a New Responsibility

4. Select the newly created responsibility (Range 01 to 08 icon) and add a range and a priority using the CHANGE RESPONSIBILITY icon () (see Figure 5.29).

Priorities for Agent Determination Rules with Responsibilities

Note that the priorities are evaluated exactly opposite the way the common enterprise language would suggest.

The highest priority is 99, and the lowest priority is 00. So if you have "priority 1" in mind, you should enter a high numeric value in the PRIORITY field.

5. In the dialog that appears, specify the value ranges for all container elements that are usually defined. In the example shown in Figure 5.28, exactly one element is defined (RuleVal).

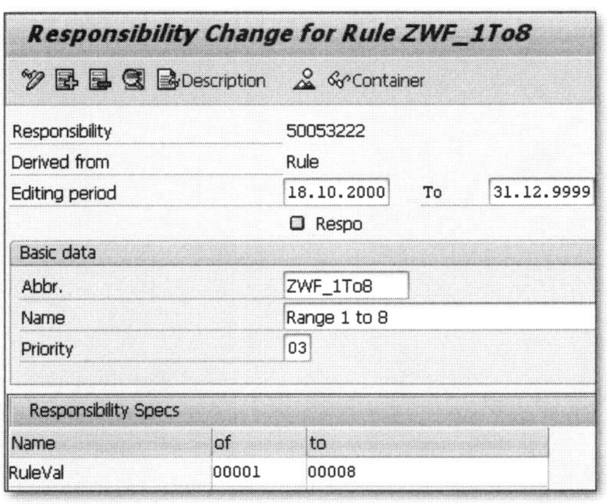

Figure 5.28 Rule Area of a Responsibility with Priority

6. Define various responsibilities with an overlapping value range to examine the effect of priorities and value ranges. For this example, you've created three responsibilities:
   - ZWF_1To8 from 00001 to 00008 with priority 03
   - ZWF_7To34 from 00007 to 00034 with priority 02
   - ZWF_TheRest from 00000 to 99999 with priority 01
7. Now click the Insert Agent Assignment icon ( ) to assign agents to each of these responsibilities. If possible, use jobs and positions from the organizational structure here. Figure 5.29 shows the responsibilities with assigned positions.

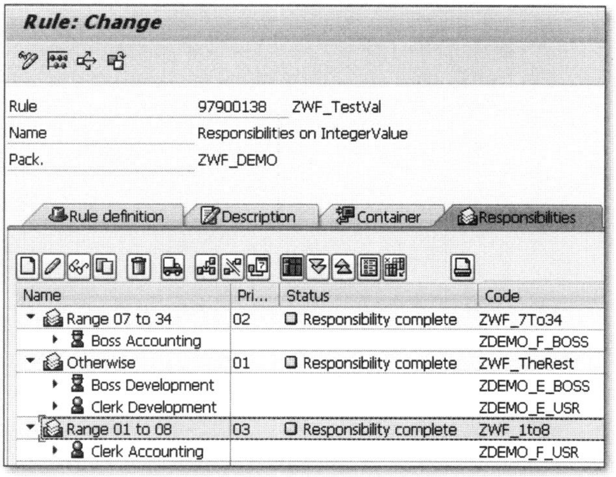

Figure 5.29 Responsibilities with Agent Assignment

8. Save ( ) your work and test the newly created rule by clicking the Simulate Rule Resolution icon ( ).

You can now use the newly created rule in the workflow environment for determining agents based on the `RuleVal` container element.

The interface for simulating a rule resolution is displayed as a separate window (see Figure 5.30). You have the option to implement an agent determination of a specific value.

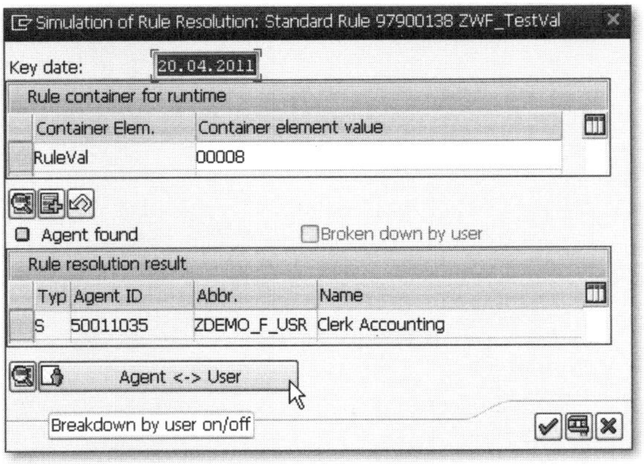

Figure 5.30 Simulating an Agent Determination with Concrete Values

Provided that the result is based on organizational units and positions, you can determine which SAP users would actually receive the work item by selecting the AGENT <-> USER button.

If you've created the rule with the same value ranges as in this example, the values 00000, 00008, 00009, and 00099 should be particularly interesting.

Save your workflow rule and the defined responsibilities by clicking the icon and, via Transaction PFTC, return to the `ZWF_RuleTest` workflow template in the Workflow Builder.

5.5.2 Integrating a Rule with the Workflow Template

Now it is time to integrate the workflow rule that is based on responsibilities with the workflow template.

1. In the detail view of the EMPTY DIALOG WITH END CONFIRMATION step (double-click on this step if not already open), select the RULE entry under AGENTS on the CONTROL tab. In the field on the right, enter the abbreviation of your rule that you've already created together with the responsibilities maintained (see Figure 5.31).

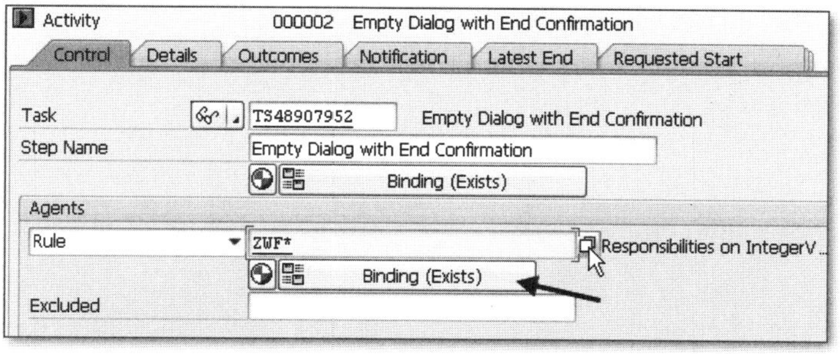

Figure 5.31 Agent Assignment Via a Rule in the Workflow Builder

2. Now establish the binding between the workflow container and the rule for the agent determination.
3. Click the DELETE LINES icon (icon) to delete possible binding instructions that may still refer to the workflow container element `&_Wf_Initiator&`.
4. Drag and drop the `RuleVal` element from the workflow container (left) to the `RuleVal` element in the rule container (right) as illustrated in Figure 5.32.

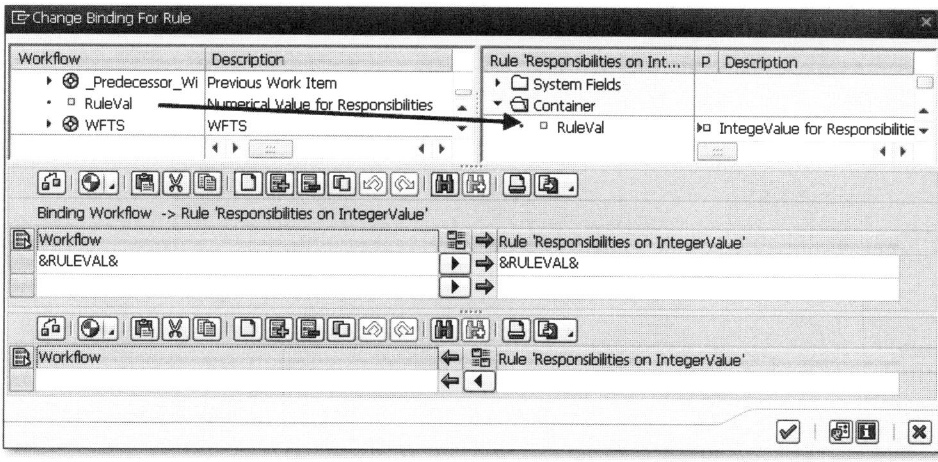

Figure 5.32 Binding Between Workflow Container and Rule Container

5. As a general practice, check the changes to the binding by clicking the CHECK BINDING icon (icon) before you exit the binding editor via the (icon) icon.
6. Now exit the detail view of this step (icon), activate the workflow template by clicking the ACTIVATE icon (icon), and then start the test environment (icon).

To test the changed binding, go back to the workflow test environment, set the mandatory container elements, and check the functionality of the workflow rule in the overall context of the workflow template.

1. Open the input area for a concrete container element by double-clicking it.
2. Enter a value for this container element (see Figure 5.33). Press [Enter] to confirm because otherwise the value is not copied to the container.
3. Refresh the organizational environment, and start the workflow by clicking the EXECUTE icon.

Now go to the WORKFLOW LOG icon and then click AGENT icon • AGENT to check whether the correct SAP users have the work item in their WORKFLOW INBOX in the workflow step (symbolized by the icon).

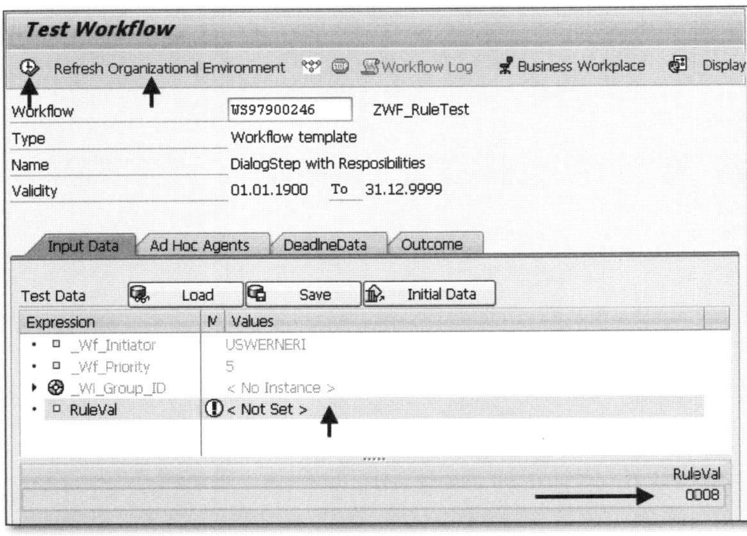

Figure 5.33 Populating a Concrete Container Element in the Workflow Test Environment

5.6 Programming the Agent Determination

In the previous section you learned that rules work with containers. You can also populate containers from an ABAP coding. That means you define a function module interface that transfers a container for an agent determination to a module.

The two most essential goals you must pursue when you design the agent determination are the following:

- Prevent the entire enterprise from receiving the work item.
- If nobody receives the work item, ensure that the modeling of the workflow template addresses this situation with deadlines or troubleshooting.

5.6.1 Creating Classic Function Modules for Agent Determination

This example provides listings you can use to determine the accounting clerk of a company code within the scope of agent determination.

Consider the `V_T001S` view or the T001S table with Transactions SE11, SE16, and SM30, which ABAP programmers know sufficiently well. You'll immediately see how a concrete SAP user is assigned to a company code and accounting clerk code (see Figure 5.34).

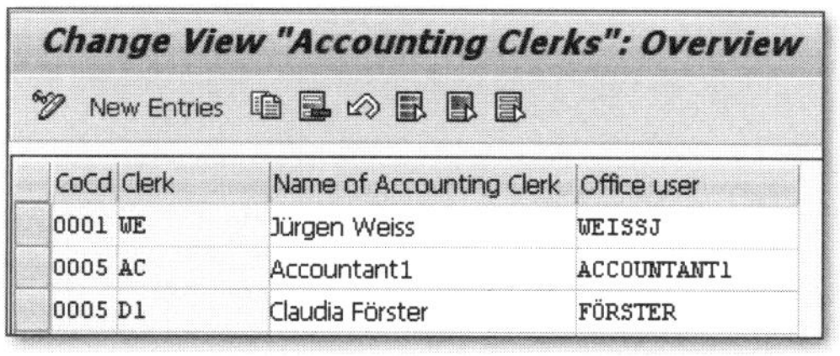

Figure 5.34 Maintenance View of "V_T001S"

To maintain this table, use the Define Accounting Clerks action in the SAP reference IMG, which is available via Transaction SPRO.

Table T001S is an excellent example of how you can maintain SAP users specifically for an application. In this table, one or more accounting clerks are assigned to a company code.

Let's assume a workflow has determined, based on its container data, that a workflow step is relevant only for a specific company code. Let's also assume that you want to address all accounting clerks for a work item.

The following three listings with classic ABAP function modules are supposed to provide support for this task.

First, you need to ensure that the Workflow Engine can handle the organizational objects determined.

An organizational object comprises a 2-digit organizational type and a 12-digit organizational object ID as they are defined in the SWHACTOR structure. Often, the combined value of this structure is used, which is a 14-digit CHAR field as it is defined in the HROBJEC_14 data type.

The organizational types relevant for the workflow are maintained in table T779O, which you can also use as a value range for domains.

Listing 5.1 shows how to use an organizational object transferred as HROBJEC_14 to specify whether it is permitted as a work item recipient. This is done by also using the RH_CHECK_ORG_OBJECT_EXISTS module in addition to the check of the object type against table T779O.

```
FUNCTION zwf_is_wf_actor.
*"----------------------------------------------------------------
*"*"Local interface:
*"  IMPORTING
*"     REFERENCE(CONCRETE_ACTOR) TYPE  HROBJEC_14
*"  EXPORTING
*"     REFERENCE(ACTOR_WF) TYPE  SWHACTOR
*"  EXCEPTIONS
*"      NO_GOOD_ACTOR
*"----------------------------------------------------------------

  DATA: lt_otypelist TYPE TABLE OF otype INITIAL SIZE 10.

  SELECT otype FROM t779o INTO TABLE lt_otypelist
         WHERE t779o~otype IS NOT NULL.

  CALL FUNCTION 'RH_CHECK_ORG_OBJECT_EXISTS'
    EXPORTING
      act_object_ext        = concrete_actor
    EXCEPTIONS
      no_active_plvar       = 1
      no_org_object         = 2
      org_object_not_found  = 3
      OTHERS                = 4.
  IF sy-subrc = 0.
    CLEAR actor_wf.
    MOVE concrete_actor(2)    TO actor_wf-otype.
```

```
    READ TABLE lt_otypelist FROM actor_wf-otype
               TRANSPORTING NO FIELDS.
    IF sy-subrc = 0.
      MOVE concrete_actor+2(12) TO actor_wf-objid.
    ELSE.
      CLEAR actor_wf.

      RAISE    no_good_actor.
    ENDIF.
  ELSE.
    CLEAR actor_wf.

    RAISE    no_good_actor.
  ENDIF.

ENDFUNCTION.
```

Listing 5.1 Module for Checking the Validity of a Workflow-Relevant Organizational Object

Next, the accounting clerks of a company code must be read and checked for their validity. Listing 5.2 shows a possible approach, which assumes that only users (US) are defined in the Customizing table.

```
FUNCTION zwf_busab_read.
*"----------------------------------------------------------------
*"*"Local interface:
*"  IMPORTING
*"     VALUE(P_BUKRS) TYPE  BUKRS OPTIONAL
*"  TABLES
*"      ACTOR_TAB STRUCTURE  SWHACTOR OPTIONAL
*"  EXCEPTIONS
*"      NO_VALID_BUSAB
*"      SENSELESS_ARGUMENTS
*"----------------------------------------------------------------


  DATA: wa_swhactor TYPE swhactor,
        wa_actor    TYPE rhobjects-object.

  CLEAR   actor_tab[].

  IF p_bukrs IS INITIAL.
```

```
    RAISE senseless_arguments.
  ENDIF.

  SELECT usnam INTO wa_swhactor-objid
         FROM   t001s
         WHERE  bukrs = p_bukrs.

    wa_swhactor-otype = 'US'.
    wa_actor          = wa_swhactor.

    CALL FUNCTION 'ZWF_IS_WF_ACTOR'
      EXPORTING
        concrete_actor = wa_actor
      IMPORTING
        actor_wf       = wa_swhactor
      EXCEPTIONS
        no_good_actor  = 1
        OTHERS         = 2.
    IF sy-subrc = 0.
      APPEND wa_swhactor TO actor_tab .
    ENDIF.

  ENDSELECT.

  IF sy-subrc <> 0 .
    RAISE no_valid_busab.
  ENDIF.

  SORT actor_tab.
  DELETE ADJACENT DUPLICATES FROM actor_tab.

ENDFUNCTION.
```

Listing 5.2 Function Module for Reading the Accounting Clerk

Let's now focus on the actual module you can use in a module-based rule in Transaction PFAC. Note that the AC_CONTAINER table with the SWCONT structure and the ACTOR_TAB table based on the SWHACTOR structure are mandatory to meet the interface specification for function module-based workflow rules.

The Workflow Engine evaluates the NOBODY_FOUND exception as the only valid exception. Listing 5.3 shows a possible module.

```
FUNCTION ZWF_BUSAB_RULE .
*"----------------------------------------------------------------------
*"*"Local interface:
*"  IMPORTING
*"     VALUE(P_BUKRS) TYPE  BUKRS OPTIONAL
*"     VALUE(P_FALLBACK) TYPE  HROBJEC_14 OPTIONAL
*"     VALUE(P_TESTCASE) TYPE  XFLAG OPTIONAL
*"  TABLES
*"      AC_CONTAINER STRUCTURE  SWCONT
*"      ACTOR_TAB STRUCTURE  SWHACTOR
*"  EXCEPTIONS
*"      NOBODY_FOUND
*"----------------------------------------------------------------------

* Import workflow macros. If necessary in function group include.
  INCLUDE <cntn01>.

  DATA: wa_swhactor TYPE swhactor.

* Ensure that a runtime container is used
  swc_container_to_runtime ac_container.

* Read elements of the container or transfer test parameter
  IF p_testcase IS INITIAL.
    CLEAR: p_bukrs, p_fallback.
    swc_get_element ac_container 'BUKRS' p_bukrs.
    swc_get_element ac_container 'FALLBACK' p_fallback.
  ENDIF.

  CALL FUNCTION 'ZWF_BUSAB_READ'
    EXPORTING
      p_bukrs              = p_bukrs
    TABLES
      actor_tab            = actor_tab
    EXCEPTIONS
      no_valid_busab       = 1
      senseless_arguments  = 2
      OTHERS               = 3.

  IF sy-subrc <> 0.
* Read elements container or transfer optional parameter
    IF NOT p_fallback IS INITIAL.
* If possible, provide an alternative.
```

```
        wa_swhactor = p_fallback.
        APPEND wa_swhactor TO actor_tab.
      ELSE.
* Only throw in nobody_found emergency
        RAISE nobody_found.
      ENDIF.
    ENDIF.

ENDFUNCTION.
```

Listing 5.3 Module for Agent Determination

Agent Determination with Classic Function Modules

Note the following tips for the agent determination with classic function modules:

- The TABLES parameters, AC_CONTAINER and ACTOR_TAB, are mandatory.
- Using additional optional parameters, you can simplify the access for the test environment and ABAP units.
- Always include a container element with a fallback user. You do this by transferring the container element &_Wf_Initiator& or another suitable container element that contains an organizational element, for example, from the workflow container.
- Generate the NOBODY_FOUND exception in case of emergency only.

After you've completed the development of a function module that meets this interface specification, you can define a rule of the AGENT DETERMINATION: FUNCTION TO BE EXECUTED type in Transaction PFAC based on the ZWF_BUSAB_RULE module.

1. To do so, create the container elements exactly as you defined them in the source code. In the example in Listing 5.3 this is BUKRS of the BUKRS type and FALLBACK of the HROBJEC_14 type.
2. Modify the workflow template defined in Listing 5.3 so that the RuleVal container element is of the BUKRS type, and change the rule's binding accordingly.
3. Transfer the &_Wf_Initiator& workflow to the rule's FALLBACK container element.

5.6.2 Creating an ABAP Class for Agent Determination

You can also use an ABAP Objects class for agent determination. This variant is available in Transaction PFAC under the option AGENT DETERMINATION: FUNCTION TO BE EXECUTED ASYNCHRONOUSLY (see Figure 5.35).

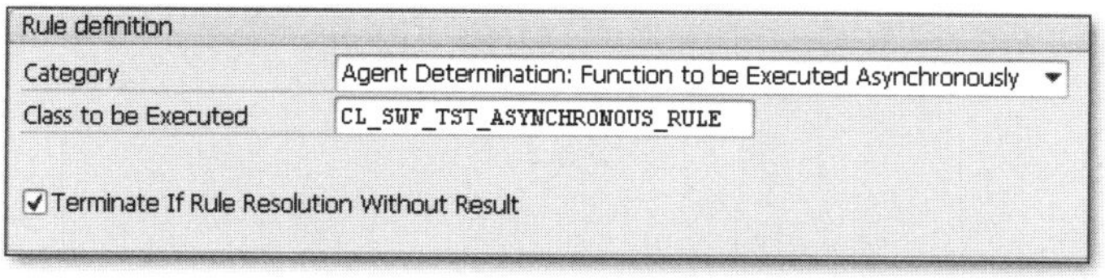

Figure 5.35 Asynchronous Agent Determination with ABAP Objects Class

Here, classes are offered for selections that implement the IF_SWF_IFS_ASYNCHRONOUS_RULE interface. This interface requires the INITIATE_EVALUATION method. The idea behind this procedure is to first generate a work item in the READY status and not assign any agents. The IF_SWF_IFS_ASYNCHRONOUS_RULE~INITIATE_EVALUATION method is then called with the work item ID of this work item and the parameter container defined in the role.

Once the agent determination has been run and the list of agents is available in a table of the SWHACTOR structures (TSWHACTOR table type), call the SAP_WAPI_ASYNC_RULE_COMPLETE function module, which forwards the agents determined to the work item using the work item API and ensures that the respective user is visible in the SAP Business Workplace (SBWP).

Because this procedure is run asynchronously, you can also involve remote systems in the agent determination. The work item remains in the correct status (READY: WITHOUT AGENT) until the WAPI methods change the work time status. In the meantime, the work item is visible in Transaction SWI2_ADM1 (Work Items without Agents).

When your agent determination requires more time or the options of an individual function module are not sufficient for agent determination, you should utilize this procedure.

Error messages during the determination of users can be collected in a message list and transferred together with the WAPI function module if required.

6 Containers, Binding, and Conditions in the Workflow

The Workflow Engine deploys *containers* for the data to be moved. A *binding* defines how the data is moved from container to container. You can specify *conditions* regarding the data in the containers to effect decisions in the workflow environment. This chapter presents the handling of these objects on the ABAP side.

The following section describes the different container types. Some listings are used as examples to show how you, as the programmer, can benefit from the workflow components.

6.1 Preparation

The Workflow Engine must transport data during the entire runtime of a workflow template, and the results of a workflow task must be made available to the next task. For example, you must temporarily store the counters of a loop and so on. The data is transported in containers, which are hierarchical key value tables that can be modified at runtime. Each value in a container must have a unique key. Also, the standard ABAP type each value involves is defined. The entire construct is then referred to as a *container element*.

A deeper structure such as tables, structures, and BOR and ABAP Objects references are possible container elements, too. It is self-explanatory that a hierarchical data format is used for saving the container between two workflow steps. Consequently, the current persistence layer of the Workflow Engine uses XML for saving the containers.

This XML persistence represents the default setting for new workflows in more recent systems. You may need to convert older transported workflows to XML persistence and retest them. For this purpose, maintain the basic data (icon) of a workflow template in the Workflow Builder. In the VERSION-DEPENDENT (CURRENT

WORKFLOW VERSION) tab, select the CONTROL tab and then the PERSISTENCE PROFILE tab. Click on the XML PERSISTENCE entry in the SETTINGS field (see Figure 6.1).

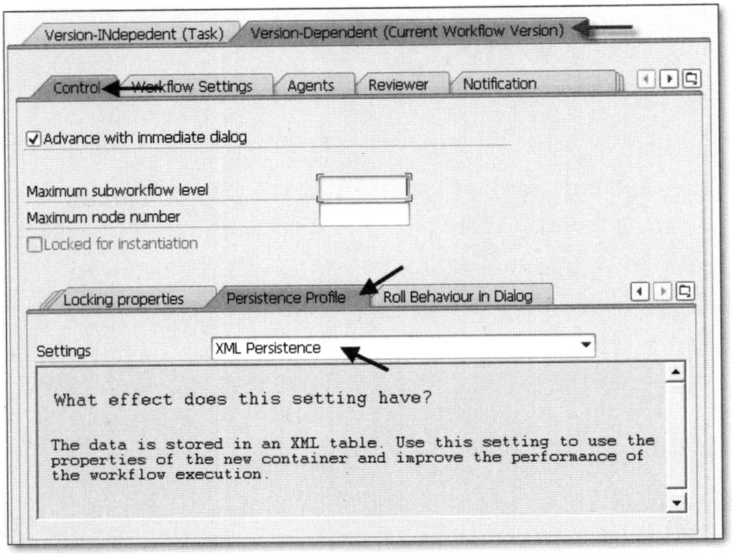

Figure 6.1 XML Persistence for Advanced Container Functionality

This setting also affects the XSLT support in the binding.

6.2 Container—Location of the Data Used by a Workflow

In the course of a workflow's lifecycle, the data required is copied multiple times between individual containers. This copy process is referred to as *binding* in the workflow environment. A binding can be defined in the customizing of a workflow or an application. It is a copy statement for container elements that can be parameterized.

Figure 6.2 shows the different types of containers and the typical hierarchy as it evolves in the course of a workflow. Every arrow represents a binding where you can define through customizing which data from the source container is required in the target container.

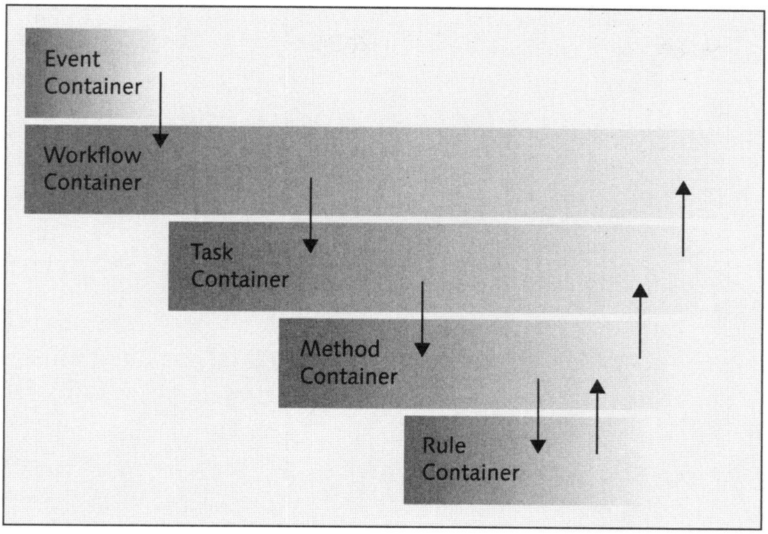

Figure 6.2 Bindings and Containers in the Typical Course of a Workflow Template

You can provide every container element with an initial value and an export or import flag. This enables you to control which elements are available for binding. There is also a MANDATORY checkbox that exists (see Figure 6.3).

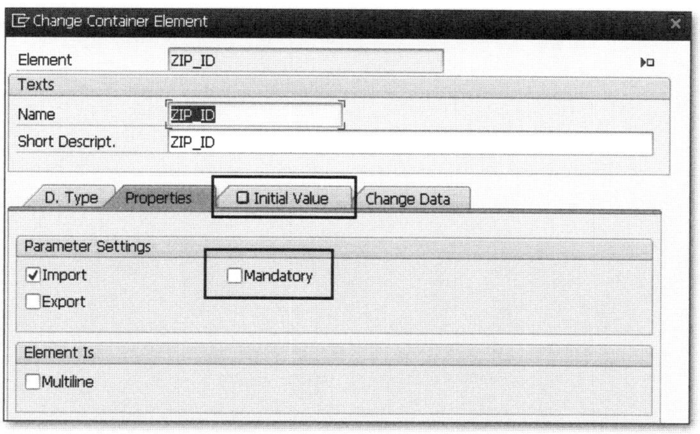

Figure 6.3 "Editor" Container Element

Container elements with the MANDATORY property must not be empty (`initial`) after the import binding because otherwise an error situation occurs.

The following subsections discuss the various container variants in their typical chronological order.

6.2.1 Event Container

An event container transports the exact key of an object instance to which it refers. Also, you can add parameters to the event container. However, the Workflow Engine only applies an export binding on an event container, which is why all container elements of an event container are implicitly export elements.

The values in an event container are set in the ABAP coding, and the event is delivered in the next update cycle on the database (ABAP statement `COMMIT WORK`). All other techniques for triggering events in the system based on change documents or system messages also populate the event container through explicit ABAP programming. You create an event container with the static method `CL_SWF_CNT_FACTORY=>CREATE_EVENT_CONTAINER` and process it with the `CL_SWF_EVT_EVENT` class.

It is beneficial to create an event with the `CL_SWF_EVT_EVENT=>RAISE_IN_UPDATE_TASK` method and the subsequent `COMMIT WORK` command if possible. This way, you ensure that you have structured relationships in the database before the Workflow Engine starts to process the events in a distributed system.

6.2.2 Workflow Container

The import binding is implemented when you start a workflow. Only container elements in the workflow container that have the IMPORT flag can be populated through the binding from the event container. When you test a workflow with Transaction SWUS, only these container elements are offered in the container editor.

The workflow container is the container with the longest persistence in the Workflow Engine. This container offers basic system variables from the SYST table for access. Moreover, there is critical runtime information about the Workflow Engine, such as the initiator of the workflow in the `_WF_INITIATOR` container element or the exact version of the running workflow template.

If you want to start a workflow template from a program, the `SWR_START_WORKFLOW` and `SAP_WAPI_START_WORKFLOW` function modules are available. The latter is an impressive starting point for the class-based programming with the `SAP Workflow-API` interface (WAPI). The SWW_WI_START and SWW_WI_START_SIMPLE function modules, which are used in older releases, are now declared obsolete (*deprecated*).

We recommend always starting the workflow template via an event if possible because you then extensively test the binding of the event containers in the workflow containers.

6.2.3 Rule Container

Before a workflow task is delivered in the dialog, it may be necessary to run a rule for agent determination. The relevant parameters are also transported via containers. The import elements of a rule container are populated from the workflow container via binding.

One specific feature of rule containers is the only container element, _RULE_RESULT, that is considered in the export binding. Because the SAP system has a defined binding here, all other container elements selected for export are ignored.

A rule container is created with the static method CL_SWF_CNT_FACTORY=>CREATE_ROLE_CONTAINER. The RH_GET_ACTOR_ATTRIBUTES_CNT function module ensures that all container elements required by the rule are available. You can then resolve a role on the basis of such a container with the RH_GET_ACTORS function module.

6.2.4 Task Container

Strictly speaking, a task—referring to the interface to the Workflow Engine—is a workflow with exactly one step. There are some historic reasons that lead to this fact. The most obvious reason is that you can embed another complete workflow template as a task within a workflow. These *subworkflows* are then logged together with the main workflow and initially behave like a regular task.

In a binding from the workflow container to a task container of a standard task or a subworkflow, you can precisely influence the quantity of data transported. Import elements are moved from the workflow container to the task container. Export elements are returned to the workflow container after the task has been performed.

You should note that you can define default rules for agent determination in a task. The container of these rules can be populated with further binding definitions from the task container.

As a programmer, you hardly ever access a task directly. Rather, you are interested in the status of a work item that is associated with this task. The SAP_WAPI interface is responsible for handling work items at runtime. This interface is discussed in more detail in Chapter 4 in the section on the SAP_WAPI interface.

For testing purposes, you should perform the individual tasks using Transaction SWUS, which involves dependent bindings in the test.

You create a task container with the static method CL_SWF_CNT_FACTORY=>CREATE_TASK_CONTAINER.

6.2.5 Method Container

The binding from the task container to the method container provides the parameters of a BOR or ABAP Objects method with data. The data transfer to these bindings is done from the task container to the method container for import parameters and vice versa for export parameters.

A method container is created with the static method CL_SWF_CNT_FACTORY=>CREATE_METHOD_CONTAINER. However, you specify the standard task into which the method is embedded as the key.

6.3 ABAP-Coding with Containers (Macros)

For ABAP programmers, the handling of containers is simplified through two measures. First, the ABAP Objects classes for direct handling of containers have been defined very powerfully. Second, you can revert to a comprehensive set of macros for functionally oriented programs and older ABAP Objects programs. It is possible to create compact and clear codes despite the handling of workflow objects.

Some facilitating macros are available to deal with containers. Depending on the programming environment, you use different includes:

- <CNTN01>: Classic function modules
- <CNTN02> <CNTN03>: ABAP Objects classes
- <SWFCNTN01>: Also within ABAP Objects class methods

The macros from the <CNTNxx> includes use function modules and static types. To be able to deploy them in the ABAP Objects field, the <CNTN01> include has to be split:

- <CNTN03>: Is integrated within the LOCAL TYPES area
- <CNTN02>: Is integrated within the MACROS area of an ABAP Objects class
- <SWFCNTN01>: Can be integrated directly within a class method if only one out of many methods must work with the container

The older macros with the swc_ prefix define the swc_container type as a table via the swcont structure. The more recent macros with the swf_ prefix define swf_container as a reference to the if_swf_cnt_container interface (see Table 6.1). As a programmer, you usually work with the CL_SWF_CNT_CONTAINER class or its interfaces IF_SWF_CNT_CONTAINER or IF_SWF_IFS_PARAMETER_CONTAINER.

Purpose	SWF Macro	SWC Macro (Classic)
Create a container data type	swf_container TYPE REF TO IF_SWF_CNT_CONTAINER	swc_container TYPE SWCONTTAB
Initialize container	swf_create_container create object type cl_swf_cnt_container	swc_create_container CLEAR/REFRESH SWCONTTAB
Clear containers	swf_clear_container CL_SWF_CNT_CONTAINER ALIAS CLEAR_ELEMENT_VALUES	swc_clear_container CLEAR/REFRESH SWCONTTAB
Determine type of container element	swf_query_element CL_SWF_CNT_CONTAINER ALIAS ELEMENT_QUERY constants in SWFCN type group	'SWC_ELEMENT_TYPEINFO_GET' function module

Table 6.1 Macros for Accessing Container Elements and BOR Objects

Purpose	SWF Macro	SWC Macro (Classic)
Set container element	swf_set_element CL_SWF_CNT_CONTAINER ALIAS ELEMENT_SET	swc_create_element swc_set_element 'SWC_ELEMENT_CREATE' and 'SWC_ELEMENT_SET' function module
Set multiline container element	swf_set_element CL_SWF_CNT_CONTAINER ALIAS ELEMENT_SET	swc_create_element swc_set_table 'SWC_ELEMENT_CREATE' and 'SWC_TABLE_SET' function module
Read container element	swf_get_element CL_SWF_CNT_CONTAINER ALIAS ELEMENT_GET	swc_get_element 'SWC_ELEMENT_GET' function module
Read multiline container element	swf_get_element CL_SWF_CNT_CONTAINER ALIAS ELEMENT_GET	swc_get_table 'SWC_TABLE_GET' function module
Delete container element	swf_delete_element CL_SWF_CNT_CONTAINER ALIAS ELEMENT_REMOVE	swc_delete_element 'SWC_ELEMENT_DELETE' function module
Copy container element	swf_copy_element CL_SWF_CNT_CONTAINER ALIAS ELEMENT_GET_DEF IF_SWF_CNT_ELEMENT METHODE SET_NAME CL_SWF_CNT_CONTAINER ALIAS ELEMENT_SET_DEF	swc_copy_element 'SWC_ELEMENT_COPY' function module
Determine BOR object type	swf_get_object_type CL_SWF_CNT_CONTAINER ALIAS GET_POR_OF_INSTANCE structure element CLASSNAME	swc_get_object_type 'SWC_OBJECT_ID_GET' function module swotobjid-objtype structure element

Table 6.1 Macros for Accessing Container Elements and BOR Objects (Cont.)

Purpose	SWF Macro	SWC Macro (Classic)
Determine BOR key attribute	swf_get_object_key CL_SWF_CNT_CONTAINER ALIAS GET_POR_OF_INSTANCE BUS_KEY structure element	swc_get_object_key 'SWC_OBJECT_ID_GET' function module swotobjid-objkey structure element
Read BOR attribute	swf_get_property For ABAP Objects, the class attribute is returned, otherwise 'SWO_INVOKE' function module is called as well	swc_get_property 'SWO_INVOKE' function module and swc_get_element macro
Read multiline BOR attribute	swf_get_property see above row	swc_get_table_property 'SWO_INVOKE' function module and swc_get_table macro
Force comparison with persistence layer	swf_refresh_object CL_SWF_CNT_CONTAINER ALIAS LOAD_FROM_DATABASE	swc_refresh_object 'SWO_OBJECT_REFRESH' function module

Table 6.1 Macros for Accessing Container Elements and BOR Objects (Cont.)

The macros in <SWFCNTN01> have been subject to changes in older releases but have been stable since SAP ECC 6.0.

6.4 ABAP Objects Classes for Handling Containers, Bindings, and Conditions

The most essential classes for handling containers include the following:

- **CL_SWF_CNT_CONTAINER**
  The RSWF_CNT_CONTAINER_DEMO report provided by SAP is the ideal entry point for using this class. This class implements all important interfaces and provides the main access to all containers in the workflow environment. The container

editor can be integrated via the CL_SWF_CNT_CONTAINER->EDIT method for testing purposes.

- **CL_SWF_CNT_ELEMENT**
  This class attends to a single container element. It is interesting for ABAP programmers whenever a container must be compiled dynamically. In this context, you should particularly note the data type editor that is available via the CL_SWF_CNT_ELEMENT->EDIT method. The option to create any container elements via the type descriptor, which is represented by the CL_ABAP_TYPEDESCR class, using the cl_swf_cnt_element=>create_by_typedescr method, makes this container highly interesting for nonworkflow applications as well.
- **CL_SWF_CNT_CONVERSION_SERVICE**
  This class provides comprehensive conversion options between different container formats. It plays a role when it is used directly, particularly for the conversion of a container's XML presentation used in the WAPI environment. Many of its functions are available via the if_swf_cnt_conversion interface directly in the CL_SWF_CNT_CONTAINER class.
- **CL_SWF_BND_BINDING**
  This class maps a binding between two containers. Here, an ABAP programmer has the option to dynamically maintain bindings in a larger, product-like workflow application within the scope of Customizing. You can integrate the binding editor with Customizing transactions using the CL_SWF_BND_EDIT_CONTROL and CL_SWF_BND_GRID_CONTROL classes. The most convenient access to the binding editor is to use the SWF_BND_BINDING_EDIT function module and store it in swfbndptab-type tables. A binding can parameterize more than just a classic MOVE statement. For example, static methods of an ABAP Objects class can be used to integrate simple operations with the binding. You can set constants and run simple addition and subtraction calculations. And—for XML persistence—you can also perform XSLT operations on container elements.
- **CL_SWF_EXP_FACTORY and CL_SWF_RLS_CONDITION**
  These two classes enable you to define dynamic conditions in Customizing and evaluate them based on container content. This adds another dynamic to the workflow development. For instance, you can use the container contents as the basis to control whether a standard task is to be executed in the background or in the dialog depending on a condition that is available in Customizing. The condition editor is available via the SWB_COND_EDIT function module. The condition is

stored in SWBCONDTAB-type tables. The evaluation of a condition is run using the SWB_COND_EVAL module, and it returns 'T' or 'F' as the result.

6.5 Coding Example for Containers, Bindings, and Conditions

The following sections describe an example that identifies the most important functions within the Workflow Engine that are the main focus of the ABAP side. This will help you to better understand the internal processes in the workflow and will motivate you to unleash the enormous potentials the Workflow Engine offers for your own projects.

6.5.1 Creating Container Elements

First, you create container elements without assigning values to them. Listing 6.1 shows how you can create container elements based on an ABAP type descriptor. Note that the container elements are initially created without reference to a container instance.

```
**** Create type descriptor for
**** DDIC structure USR01
DATA: l_typedescr
          TYPE REF TO cl_abap_typedescr,
      l_typename
          TYPE        char255.

  l_typename = 'USR01'.

  TRY.
    l_typedescr =
    cl_abap_typedescr=>describe_by_name(
                            l_typename ).
    CATCH cx_root.
  ENDTRY.
  CHECK NOT l_typedescr IS INITIAL.

**** Create container element based
**** on a type descriptor
```

```
DATA: l_cnt_elem_usr01_def
        TYPE REF TO if_swf_cnt_element.

l_cnt_elem_usr01_def = cl_swf_cnt_factory=>create_container_element(
         element_name = 'CURRENT_USER'
         typedescr    = l_typedescr
                                ).
**** Call type editor for
**** container elements
  l_cnt_elem_usr01_def->edit( ).
```

Listing 6.1 Creating Container Elements Based on an ABAP Type Descriptor

You can also create a container element based on a data reference. Listing 6.2 details this variant.

```
**** Create container element based
**** on a data reference
DATA: l_cnt_elem_tstval_def
        TYPE REF TO if_swf_cnt_element,
      l_tstval_ref
        TYPE REF TO data,
      l_tstval
        TYPE numc5.

GET REFERENCE OF l_tstval
            INTO l_tstval_ref.

l_cnt_elem_tstval_def =
  cl_swf_cnt_factory=>create_container_element(
          element_name = 'TEST_VALUE'
          data_ref     = l_tstval_ref
                ).
**** Call type editor for
**** container elements
  l_cnt_elem_tstval_def->edit( )
```

Listing 6.2 Creating Container Elements Based on a Data Reference

The `edit` method on a container element takes you to the data type editor. Here you can re-edit the container element's definition (see Figure 6.4).

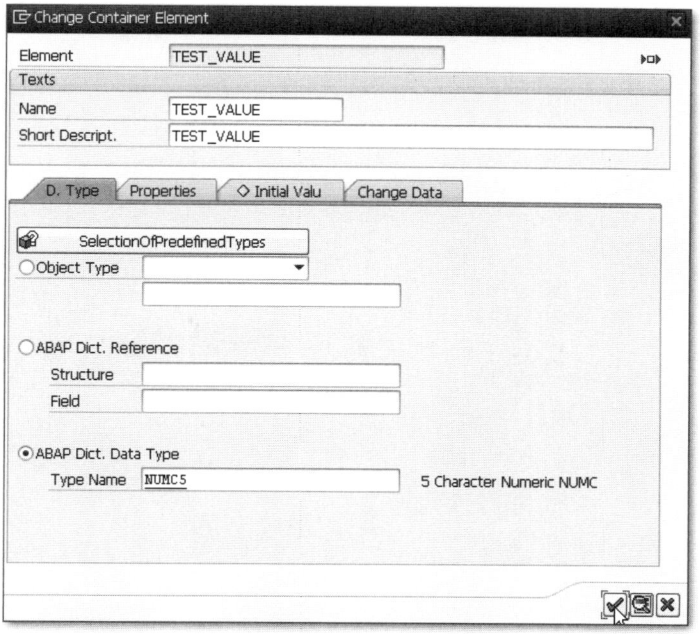

Figure 6.4 Data Type Editor for Container Elements

6.5.2 Creating Containers

You now subordinate the container elements you just created (see Listing 6.3). Here, the container elements are created initially. No values are transferred. The container elements are selected for export in the "source container" so you can use them later in a binding.

```
**** Create an empty container
DATA: l_cnt_if
       TYPE REF TO if_swf_cnt_container.
CREATE OBJECT l_cnt_if
         TYPE cl_swf_cnt_container.

**** Integrate container elements
**** via definition (without value)
DATA: l_cnt_elem_usr01
       TYPE REF TO if_swf_cnt_element,
      l_cnt_elem_tstval
       TYPE REF TO if_swf_cnt_element.
```

```
l_cnt_if->set_element_def(
    EXPORTING
      element     = l_cnt_elem_usr01_def
    IMPORTING
      new_element = l_cnt_elem_usr01
         ).

l_cnt_if->set_element_def(
   EXPORTING
     element     = l_cnt_elem_tstval_def
   IMPORTING
     new_element = l_cnt_elem_tstval
         ).
**** Select container elements
**** for export
l_cnt_elem_usr01->set_props(
       properties = swfcn_p_param_export
                              ).
l_cnt_elem_tstval->set_props(
       properties = swfcn_p_param_export
                              ).
```

Listing 6.3 Create Empty Container and Copy Element Definitions

Now it is time to populate the container elements with values. In the following example, you populate one of your container elements with values from the result of a selection (see Listing 6.4).

```
** Set value of a container element
DATA: wa_usr01 TYPE usr01.
   select single * into wa_usr01
      from usr01
      where BNAME = USERNAME.

l_cnt_elem_usr01->set_value(
                     value = wa_usr01 ).

**** Call container editor and
**** set further values.
l_cnt_if->edit(
    EXPORTING
      display_only  = space
```

```
    editor_title   = 'Test Container'
      ).
```

Listing 6.4 Setting Element Values and Calling the Container Editor

The `edit` method in the ABAP-OO class describing a container takes you to the container editor (see Figure 6.5). You can change the container elements here. You already know the editor's behavior from Transaction SWUS. Double-click the container element to be changed to select it. Then confirm the changed values by pressing the Enter key to accept them.

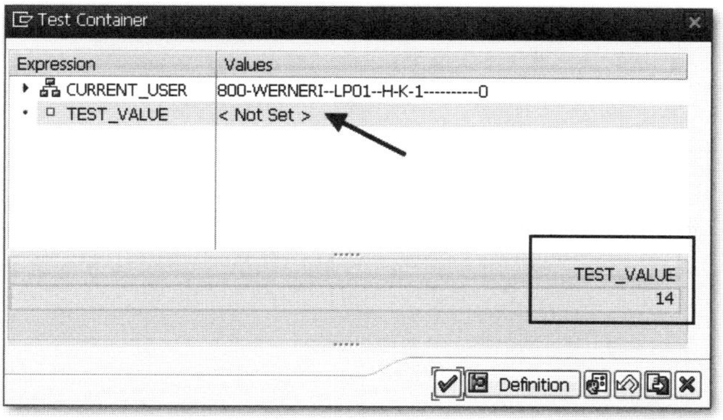

Figure 6.5 Container Editor for Editing the Contents of a Container

6.5.3 Converting Containers

The conversion between container types is a routine procedure in the workflow environment. Listing 6.5 shows the conversion of a class-based container into the table-like presentation in the BOR environment.

```
**** Data retention for BOR container
DATA: t_contval   TYPE swconttab,
      t_contdef   TYPE swbconttab.

**** Run container conversion
l_cnt_if->
 if_swf_cnt_conversion~to_bor_container(
    IMPORTING
      values      = t_contval
```

```
      definition   = t_contdef
         ).
```

Listing 6.5 Conversion of a Container into the BOR Format

6.5.4 Creating Workflow Conditions

You can utilize the container's definition in the BOR presentation to create a workflow condition. Listing 6.6 shows how to call the condition editor and applies this condition immediately to the container.

```
**** Create workflow condition
DATA: t_condition
        TYPE swb_cond
        OCCURS 0 WITH HEADER LINE.

CALL FUNCTION 'SWB_COND_EDIT'
  EXPORTING
    condition_name = 'TEST Condition'
  TABLES
      contdef       = t_contdef[]
      condition     = t_condition[].

**** Evaluate workflow condition
  DATA:  l_cond_result TYPE sybinpt.
  CALL FUNCTION 'SWB_COND_EVAL'
    EXPORTING
      container_if = l_cnt_if
    IMPORTING
      RESULT        = l_cond_result
    TABLES
      condition     = t_condition[].

  CHECK l_cond_result = 'T'.
```

Listing 6.6 Creating and Evaluating a Workflow Condition

Figure 6.6 shows the condition editor. Here you can compile logical expressions based on container content and save them in Customizing of a workflow application if required.

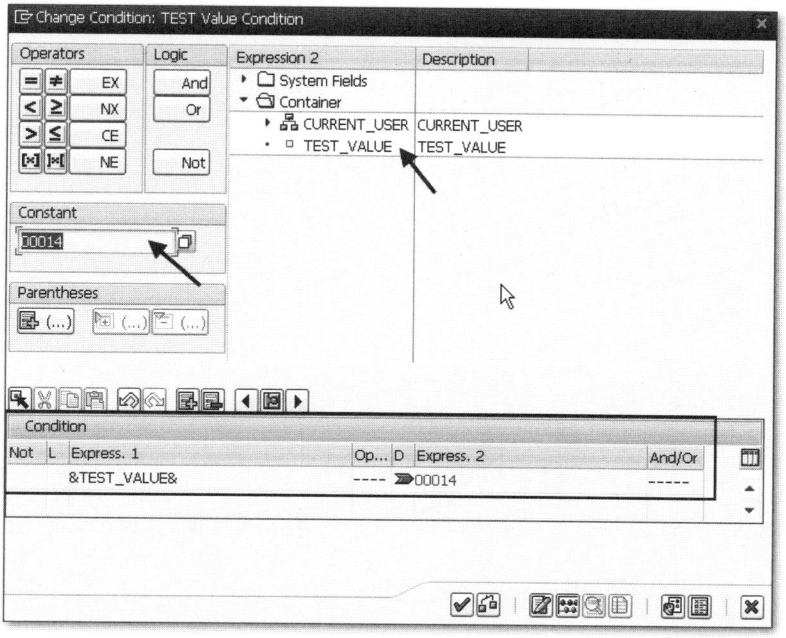

Figure 6.6 Condition Editor for Workflow Conditions

For subsequent use in a binding, you now create another container for this example. This time, you create the container elements directly with the values in the container instance. In Listing 6.7, the properties of the container elements are set in such a way that the Workflow Engine allows their usage in an import binding. The constant bit patterns for the properties are located in the `SWFCN` type group.

```
**** Create container (with values)
DATA: l_out_cnt_if
        TYPE REF TO if_swf_cnt_container.
CREATE OBJECT l_out_cnt_if
         TYPE cl_swf_cnt_container.

DATA: intval    TYPE int4 VALUE 99,
      usrval    TYPE usr01,
      usrref    TYPE REF TO data,
      keyvaltab TYPE scol_key_value_t,
      keyvalref TYPE REF TO data.

GET REFERENCE OF keyvaltab
            INTO keyvalref.
```

```
l_out_cnt_if->element_set_ref(
                name   = 'KeyValPairs'
                value_ref = keyvalref ).

GET REFERENCE OF usrval
            INTO usrref.

  l_out_cnt_if->element_set_ref(
                name   = 'TheUser'
                value_ref = usrref ).

  l_out_cnt_if->element_set(
                name   = 'OutInteger'
                value = intval ).

**** Select container elements
**** for import
DATA:
l_props_import_optional type SWFDBITS64.

l_props_import_optional =
       swfcn_p_param_import   BIT-OR
       swfcn_p_param_optional.

l_out_cnt_if->element_set_props(
    name       = 'KeyValPairs'
    properties = l_props_import_optional
       ).

l_out_cnt_if->element_set_props(
   name        = 'TheUser'
   properties  = swfcn_p_param_import
       ).

l_out_cnt_if->element_set_props(
   name       = 'OutInteger'
   properties = swfcn_p_param_import
       ).
```

Listing 6.7 Creating Container Elements with Values

6.5.5 Defining the Binding

Listing 6.8 shows the simplest variant to call the binding editor. Depending on the participating containers, a binding can define both the export time and the import time. In this example, you only use the export and therefore set the `'E'` flag in the `dataflow` parameter.

```
**** Define binding for export
DATA: l_binding_def
          TYPE swfbndptab,
      l_binding
          TYPE REF TO cl_swf_bnd_binding.

CALL FUNCTION 'SWF_BND_BINDING_EDIT'
  EXPORTING
    swf_binding      = l_binding_def
    source_container = l_cnt_if
    target_container = l_out_cnt_if
  IMPORTING
    new_swf_binding  = l_binding_def.

CREATE OBJECT l_binding
         TYPE cl_swf_bnd_binding.

l_binding->set_persistent_binding(
              swf_binding = l_binding_def
         ).
l_binding->set_source_container(
              dataflow = 'E'
              source_container = l_cnt_if
         ).
l_binding->set_target_container(
              dataflow = 'E'
              target_container =
                          l_out_cnt_if
         ).
```

Listing 6.8 Calling the Binding Editor and Creating the Binding Object

Figure 6.7 shows the binding editor with a populated export page. In this editor you can define the binding using drag-and-drop:

- Drag-and-drop from left to right defines the import binding.
- Drag-and-drop from right to left defines the export binding.

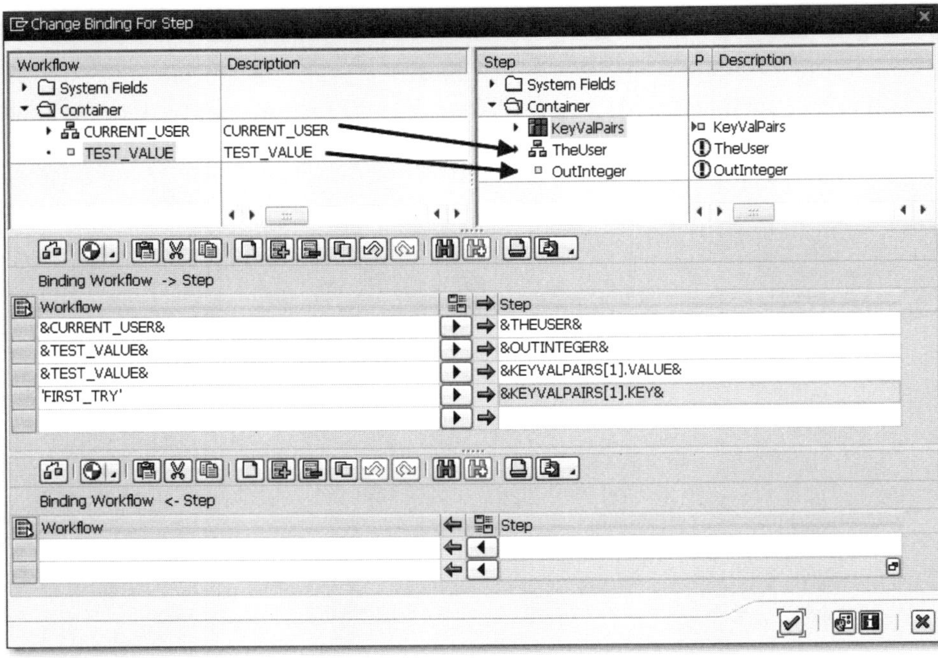

Figure 6.7 Binding Editor

Listing 6.9 runs the binding when the binding debugger is activated:

```
**** Activate binding debugger
CALL FUNCTION 'SWU_SET_USER_FLAG'
    EXPORTING
      index = 1
      flag  = 'X'.

**** Execute binding
  l_binding->execute(
    EXPORTING
      dataflow       = 'E'
         ).

  l_out_cnt_if->edit(
      EXPORTING
        display_only  = 'X'
        editor_title  = 'Test Output Container'
           ).
```

Listing 6.9 Binding with Activated Binding Debugger

The container editor in the display mode shows the result of the binding (see Figure 6.8).

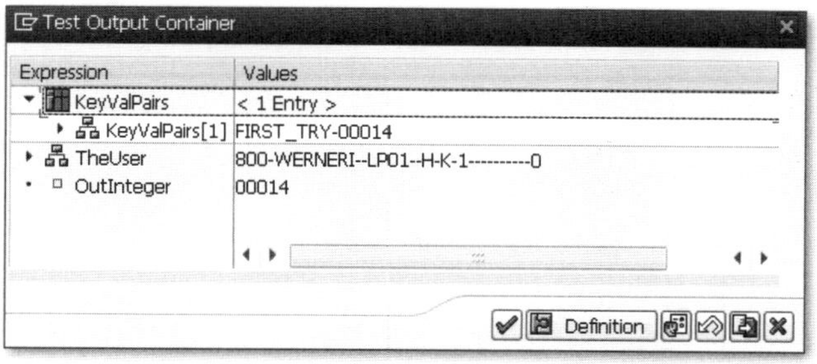

Figure 6.8 Container Editor in Display Mode with Results

The binding debugger tries to visualize the contents of the container directly after the binding (see Figure 6.9).

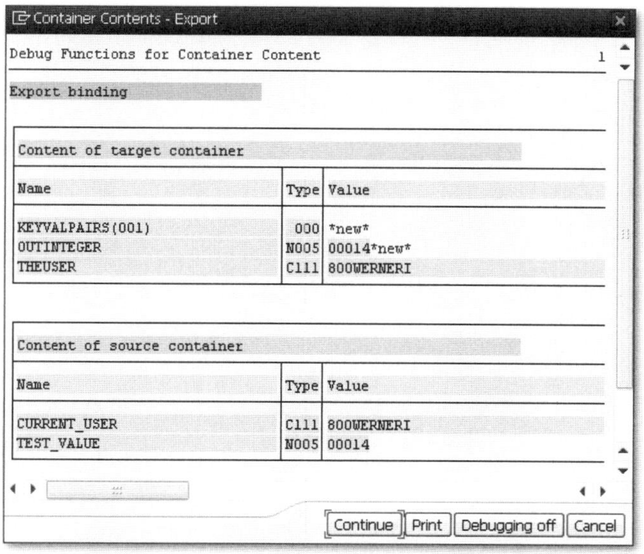

Figure 6.9 Binding Debugger for Simple Operations

If the binding debugger is a useful tool for you, you can force it to be switched on by default by using Transaction SWUS under GOTO • OPTIONS. Select ASYNCHRONOUS EXECUTION USING ARFC as the DEBUG MODE. Figure 6.10 shows the precise settings.

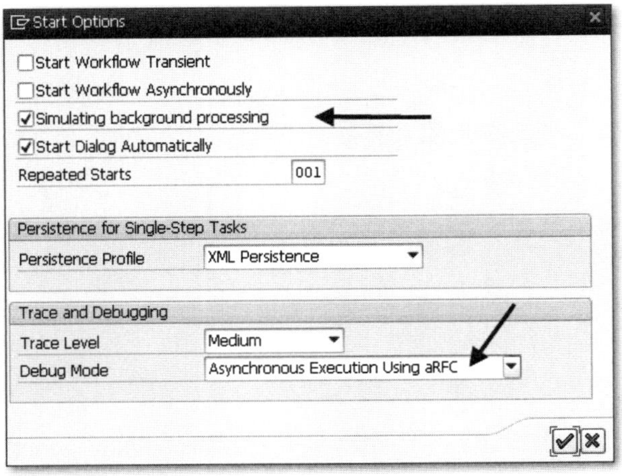

Figure 6.10 Transaction SWUS—Activating the Binding Debugger

6.6 Advanced Functionality in the Binding

Within the binding you can use an advanced functionality. Table 6.2 shows an overview of the syntactical options in the binding editor.

Syntax	Effect
`&table[index]&`	Addressing a table row
`&table[index].column&`	Addressing a column in a table row
`&table[].column&`	An entire column of a table as a multirow element
`&table1[1].table2[2]&`	Hierarchical addressing of a table in a table
`&object.get_value( )&`	Instance method without parameter
`&object.methodeXY ( param1=&exp1&; param2=4711 )&`	Instance method with parameters, which can also be binding expressions
`%classname.static_method ( param1=&exp& )%`	Static method of a class

Table 6.2 Syntactical Options in the Binding

6.7 Programmed Binding

If all else fails and you are in a situation where calling functional methods is no longer sufficient to implement a special binding, you still have the option to program a binding.

For this purpose, you must define ABAP Objects classes that implement the `IF_SWF_IFS_BIND_TRANSFORM` interface for bindings from expression to expression or the `IF_SWF_IFS_BIND_TRANSFORM_CONT` interface for bindings from container to container. Both interfaces define the `CHECK`, `TRANSFORM`, and `GET_SUPPORTED_OPTIONS` methods.

The classes that implement these interfaces are shown as enhancements in the binding editor's options menu (see Figure 6.11).

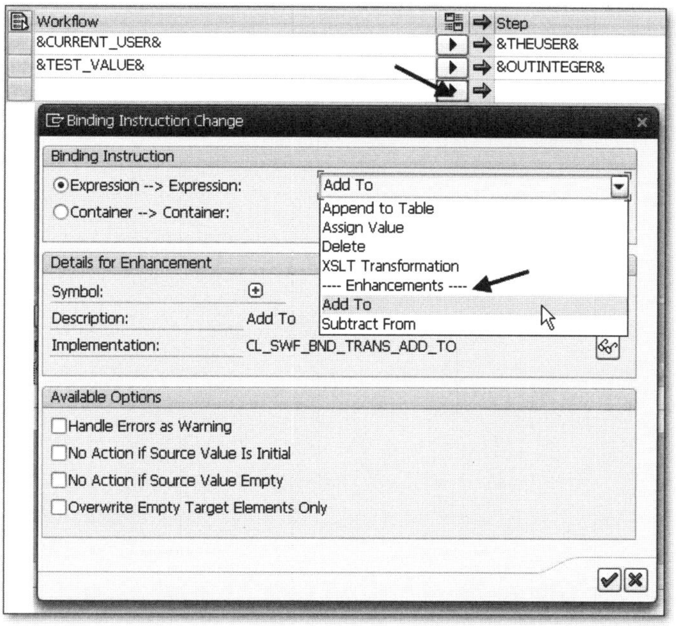

Figure 6.11 Programmed Binding with ABAP Objects Classes

In Transaction SE80 you should closely examine the source code of the sample classes `CL_SWF_BND_TRANS_ADD_TO` and `CL_SWF_BND_TRANS_SUBTRACT_FROM`, which are provided by SAP. How these classes are presented in the binding editor is controlled via the IF_SWF_IFS_BIND_PRESENTATION interface, which provides the binding editor with the GET_ICON, GET_NAME, and GET_DESCRIPTION methods.

The application log and the workflow trace are provided for debugging in these class-based enhancements for the binding editor.

Specifically for the binding from container to container, you still have the option to implement a binding via a function module. This variant in ECC 6.0 releases exists also with the new object-oriented container interface. A function module for the binding must be copied from the SWA_BINDING_TEMPLATE sample function module and enhanced (see Figure 6.12).

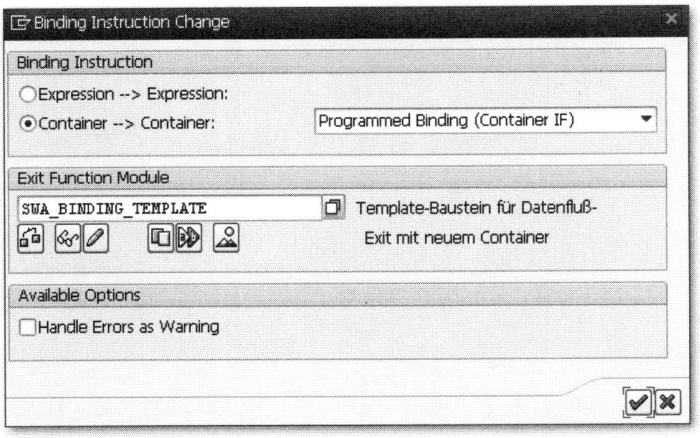

Figure 6.12 Programmed Binding via Function Module with New Container Interface

You should use this procedure only if this is absolutely unavoidable. The debug options are limited, and the error analysis of failure somewhere in some binding is elaborate.

Special Container Elements

Some container elements are automatically filled by the Workflow Engine in specific situations and used internally.

- In an event container, the &_EVT_OBJECT& container element always includes a reference to the triggering object. The &_EVT_CREATOR& element includes the user ID of the user that triggered the event.
- The &_WF_INITIATOR& container element is always set in a workflow container. There's a default binding from the &_EVT_CREATOR& element to the &_WF_INITIATOR& element in case of triggering events.

- Every task container has a &_WI_OBJECT_ID& variable for the object reference to which the task refers. The task assumes that the object type of this reference is the reference that was specified when the task was defined. Usually, this variable is copied back in the binding after the task has been performed.
- For the binding from the task container to the workflow container, the &_WI_ACTUAL_AGENT& element includes the ID of the user who just performed the task.
- The &_RULE_RESULT& container element of the AAGENT BOR type contains the result of the agent determination for this special task.

7 Sample Project—Designing an ABAP Objects Class for the Workflow

ABAP Objects classes are not readily suitable for use in the workflow environment. This chapter describes the minimum work required to meet the Workflow Engine requirements for an ABAP Objects class.

The goal of this chapter is to create a workflow-compliant ABAP Objects class whose methods can be integrated with standard tasks and can therefore be used in the workflow.

7.1 Initial Situation

For some years, the SAP standard has provided a well-equipped ABAP Objects class called `CL_ABAP_ZIP` for working with zip files. There is no classic BOR object and no workflow-compliant ABAP Objects class for this class. We create the BOR object in Chapter 8; the following sections focus on the more modern ABAP Objects-oriented approach.

Let's assume that a zip file is to be processed within the scope of a workflow. Files are supposed to be moved via SAP GUI upload and SAP GUI download from and to the zip file. The zip file itself is supposed to be persisted. The database entries that are created within the scope of this persistence are to be removed later.

The functionality for handling the zip file is implemented by various public methods within the ABAP Objects class `CL_ABAP_ZIP`. You now want to extend this class in such a way that it can be directly used by the Workflow Engine.

The *key* is the most obvious difference between "normal" ABAP Objects classes and BOR objects in the workflow. Every instance of an object in the workflow must be identifiable as a key via a character string (`CHAR` data type). Ideally, you should never be able to instantiate the class without this key. This key can have up to 32 characters for ABAP Objects classes in the workflow (it is shorter than in the BOR environment). The Workflow Engine uses the `SIBFLPOR` structure internally.

Frequently, the 32-character presentation of the *object GUID* of a persistent class is used as the workflow key. Such a GUID is an artificial key that is unique in every system. Using the `IF_OS_CA_PERSISTENCY~GET_PERSISTENT_BY_KEY` method, you can use this GUID then to instantiate a corresponding persistent class as well, implementing more complex queries in the database if the persistent class is not a simple select. With the `GET_OID_BY_REF` and `GET_REF_BY_OID` methods in the `IF_OS_CA_SERVICE` interface you can determine the object GUID on the basis of the object reference at runtime. In the class design, you should nevertheless avoid directly using persistent classes by extending them with the IF_WOKRFLOW interface. Rather, you should use three classes: one for the business logic, one for the provision in the workflow, and a third one for the persistence.

Trick for Using Longer Key Structures

A frequently used trick to implement key structures with more than 32 characters is to serialize a strongly typed DDIC structure in a short XML string, to build the MD5 hash of this XML string, and to use it as a GUID (and thus divert it from its intended use). You probably know an MD5 hash as the cross total for downloads from the Internet. Its purpose is to obtain a unique identification key for a random binding. So you import your key structure when you search for the persistence via a database SELECT command and convert this structure via an XML string into a unique technical key:

- Convert data structure into an XML object with the `CREATE_WITH_DATA` method of the `CL_XML_DOCUMENT` ABAP Objects class.
- Write the XML object to a string with the `RENDER_2_XSTRING` method of the `CL_XML_DOCUMENT` ABAP Objects class.
- Calculate the MD5 hash with the CALCULATE_HASH_FOR_RAW function module.

Another important difference (besides the constraint of a unique key) is the fact that the persistence cycles of the Workflow Engine do not necessarily concur with the lifecycle of an ABAP Objects class.

Because the Workflow Engine only persists the key and not an object reference, another challenge arises: You must ensure that the system can re-create the state that existed before the persistence process through a reinitialization with the unique key after a "break."

If your business functionality also depends on instances of additional ABAP Objects class instances, you should implement an instance management. Therefore, these classes do not have to run through the constructor again (which is slightly elaborate) because the Workflow Engine persists from time to time. Thanks to this procedure, you still have a class reference in your instance management, and the garbage collector doesn't clean up unnecessarily.

7.2 Specific Features in the Workflow Environment

The Workflow Engine requires a default attribute and a default method.

- The *default attribute* is displayed in logs and texts whenever an instance of the object is referenced. In many cases, the unique key or a text presentation of it is also the default attribute.
- The *default method* is called if a link to the object is triggered by a user action; for instance, by double-clicking a link in the SAP Business Workplace. Usually, the default method is a `DISPLAY` method, which calls the relevant transaction for viewing the object.

The support in workflow design tools should be mentioned as the last specific feature besides the default attribute and the default method. For instance, the binding editor looks up the methods, their parameters, and the attributes only in the Data Dictionary (DDIC) without forming an instance of the class used. Consequently, you should work with complete typing if you use references to other ABAP Objects classes in attributes.

Consider which functionality you want to provide in the workflow, and implement all of these functions as a `public` method in your class. The methods should have simple parameter sets so that the binding in the workflow doesn't get too complex.

To create an ABAP Objects class for use in the workflow, follow these instructions:

1. **Ensure core functionality**
   Ensure that the core functionality is already available in "normal" classes. The class you provide for the workflow only bundles the functionality of the "normal" classes for the Workflow Engine. Implement the `IF_WORKFLOW` interface in this class so that the Workflow Engine recognizes it.
2. **Create exception classes**
   Always create two exception classed based on the SAP Standard exception classes `CX_BO_ERROR` and `CX_BO_TEMPORARY`. Maintain the error texts of these exception classes in an ABAP message class. This facilitates the translation of error texts and makes them available in the classic parts of your application.

3. **Implement instance management**
   As soon as you use additional nonworkflow classes (that is, virtually all of the time), you must implement an instance management. For this purpose, you can use persistent classes or possibly an instance list that is maintained as a static attribute and linked with an XML serialization and a data cluster (see Listing 7.7).
4. **Define key attributes**
   Define the key attributes and ensure that these simple character strings have a fixed length (CHAR-like). The total length of all key attributes must not exceed 32 characters. If this key length is not sufficient, you must revert to a GUID as an artificial key. Then assign the entire key of this GUID via a help table or an MD5 hash.
5. **Specify the technical instantiation**
   Don't leave the lifecycle exclusively to the interaction of the constructor and garbage collector. Set the technical instance creation of your class to PRIVATE (see Figure 7.2) and offer static class methods that explicitly create or destroy instances considering the key attributes or GUIDs (factory methods).
6. **Create persistence layer**
   Ensure that a persistence layer exists. If the database layer and the user interface are not yet ready during the development, assign the IF_SERIALIZABLE_OBJECT interface to your class. This enables you to serialize and deserialize the data areas of your class in an XML presentation. An XML presentation as the "display" mode may suffice until the user interface of your workflow class is completed.

7.3 Creating a Class, Integrating IF_WORKFLOW, and Defining Key Attributes

Because you've declared the CL_ABAP_ZIP class as final, you cannot avoid either creating a copy of this class or providing it in an ABAP Objects class for the workflow to be developed anew. To avoid missing any future updates from SAP or other components, the second option is definitely preferable.

In the following instructions, you create a ZCL_WF_ZIP class that presents a zip file for each instance in the workflow. Later, you can implement a list of files that are included in the zip file as the attributes in the workflow to display this overview if required. You can also display a checksum to determine status changes of the zip file. You can use an MD5 hash as the cross total. This hash is calculated with the CALCULATE_HASH_FOR_RAW function module.

1. Create the ZCL_WF_ZIP class (Zip Utility workflow) in Transaction SE80.
2. Integrate the IF_WORKFLOW interface.
3. After you save the new class for the first time, ensure that the ATTRIBUTES tab offers an additional column, KEY ATTRIBUTE.
4. Create a ZIP_ID key attribute of the GUID_32 type for your example (see Figure 7.1).

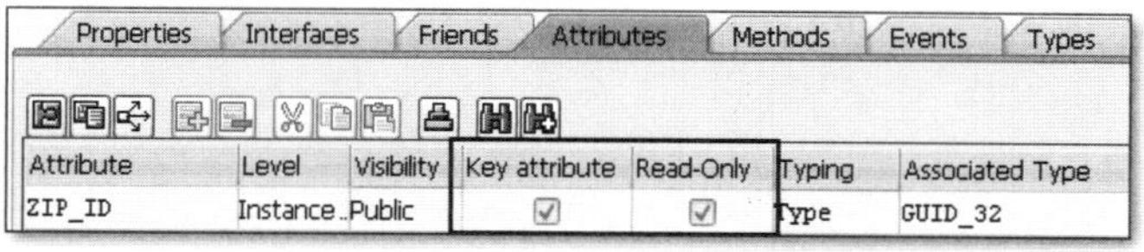

Figure 7.1 "IF_WORKFLOW" Interface—Defining Key Attributes

It is obvious why a GUID is used as the key attribute here: You cannot identify a zip file based on a real key. Where the zip file comes from is not important for the system—whether from the frontend or from a server directory. In other words, you don't have to create an artificial key that represents a "loaded zip file" in the system and is unique across the system.

You can use the GUID_CREATE function module to create such an artificial, system-wide unique ID.

Let's now go over the individual methods required by the IF_WORKFLOW interface:

- **BI_PERSISTENT~FIND_BY_LPOR**
  The Workflow Engine calls this static method if a running instance of the ABAP Objects class is required and only the key is currently available. Transfer the SIBFLPOR structure here, which contains the following elements:
  - Object category CATID ("CL" or "BO")
  - Object type TYPEID (name of the class or the BOR object)
  - Field INSTID as the key (up to 32 characters long)

  It is your task to ensure that the system returns a class reference based on the key in the INSTID field. You can find more information on this topic in Section 7.4.

- **BI_PERSISTENT~LPOR**
  This instance method returns a SIBFLPOR structure. This is when the Workflow Engine releases the class reference that points to an ABAP Objects class. Later, it again obtains a reference to the class using the BI_PERSISTENT~FIND_BY_LPOR method.
- **BI_PERSISTENT~REFRESH**
  Using this instance method, the Workflow Engine prompts the ABAP Objects class to update all visible attributes. Here, attributes in particular must be recalculated or reread by the database.
- **BI_OBJECT~DEFAULT_ATTRIBUTE_VALUE**
  This method returns the value of the attribute that is supposed to be integrated with work item texts and links when reference is made to the object. Usually the default attribute is a single-line presentation of the key.
- **BI_OBJECT~EXECUTE_DEFAULT_METHOD**
  The Workflow Engine calls this method to trigger the default functionality within the class. Usually, the object identified by the key is displayed. This can be the responsible maintenance transaction in "real" business objects. At development time it is sufficient to display the most critical attributes of the class.

  This instance method is called when you double-click an object reference within the Workflow Engine.
- **BI_OBJECT~RELEASE**
  With this instance method, the Workflow Engine grants the "license to clean up." Any shared memory objects, dependent class instances, or temporary database entries must be left in such a way that the garbage collector of the ABAP Objects engine removes the class and its memory used in its next run. This is only a "technical cleanup." You must not touch the database tables that contain your business object.

7.4 Managing and Creating Instances

Previously, you learned that you require an instance management for ABAP Objects classes in the workflow. The reason for this is the continuous change between a persistent object reference (POR) and a real ABAP Objects runtime reference when you reference your class.

If you passed the constructor for every new request of a runtime reference via the `BI_PERSISTENT~FIND_BY_LPOR` method, reimported all attributes that are based on the database, and reinstantiated all logically dependent classes, you would unnecessarily occupy the system with object creation and garbage collection. This definitely cannot be intentional. You must put exactly one reference of the class per key aside and keep it until the Workflow Engine calls the `BI_OBJECT~RELEASE` method. In this way, you prevent the ABAP Objects garbage collector from removing the class prematurely from the memory.

A suitable location to keep such a list of class instances is a static table of structures that you use to link the `INSTID` field of the `LPOR` structure with a class reference (`REF TO` variable) that refers to the appropriate class instance in the memory.

1. You can start with a class-based type, for example. Here you link the key and the class reference. Create a table of this type in the static memory area of the class (see Listing 7.1).

```
types:
      begin of t_instance,
       guid     type        guid_16,
       instance type ref to zcl_wf_zip,
      end of t_instance .
types:
 t_instances type standard table
       of t_instance with default key .
class-data  mst_instances type t_instances .
```

Listing 7.1 Static Table for Keeping Class Instances over the Workflow Lifecycle

2. In the **Properties** tab, set the technical instantiation of your class to "Private" in the **Instantiation** field (see Figure 7.2).

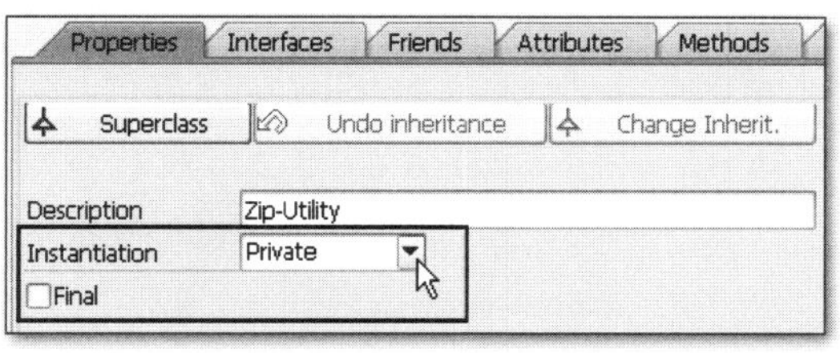

Figure 7.2 Setting the Technical Instantiation to "Private"

With this setting you prevent the constructor from being called directly from the outside, which creates instances of the class that are not included in your instance management table.

3. You can now provide a public static method GET_INSTANCE (see Figure 7.3), which returns an already known instance based on the key or, if requested, creates a new instance and adds it to the list (see Listing 7.2).

Ty.	Parameter	Type spec.
▸□	VALUE(ZIP_ID)	TYPE GUID_16 OPTIONAL
□▸	VALUE(RE_ZIP_CLASS)	TYPE REF TO ZCL_WF_ZIP

Figure 7.3 "GET_INSTANCE" Signature

```
METHOD get_instance.
  DATA: l_lpor   TYPE sibflpor,
        l_guid16 TYPE guid_16.

* Create key
  IF zip_id IS INITIAL.
    CALL FUNCTION 'GUID_CREATE'
      IMPORTING
        ev_guid_16 = l_guid16.
    l_lpor-instid  = l_guid16.
  ELSE.
    l_lpor-instid = zip_id.
  ENDIF.

* Fill LPOR structure
  l_lpor-catid  = 'CL'.
  l_lpor-typeid = 'ZCL_WF_ZIP'.

* Call find_by_lpor
  re_zip_class ?= zcl_wf_zip=>
   bi_persistent~find_by_lpor( l_lpor ).

ENDMETHOD.
```

Listing 7.2 Signature and Coding of a "GET_INSTANCE" Method

You have probably noticed that the method for instance creation assumes the Workflow Engine role. Finally, call the BI_PERSISTENT~FIND_BY_LPOR method (see Figure 7.4). This is a useful trick because you then obtain a correct class reference in the test environment while simultaneously testing the code that you provide to the Workflow Engine (see Listing 7.3).

Ty.	Parameter	Type spec.
	LPOR	TYPE SIBFLPOR
	VALUE(RESULT)	TYPE REF TO BI_PERSISTENT

Figure 7.4 "bi_persistent~find_by_lpor" Signature

```
METHOD bi_persistent~find_by_lpor.
  DATA: l_instance  TYPE t_instance,
        l_zip_id    TYPE guid_16.

*  CHECK lpor-instid IS INITIAL.

  l_zip_id = lpor-instid.
  READ TABLE mst_instances WITH KEY
    guid = l_zip_id INTO l_instance.
  IF sy-subrc <> 0.

    l_instance-guid = l_zip_id.
  TRY.
     CREATE OBJECT l_instance-instance
        EXPORTING
           zip_id = l_zip_id.
        CATCH cx_bo_error.
            EXIT.
  ENDTRY.
    APPEND l_instance TO mst_instances.
  ENDIF.

  result = l_instance-instance.
ENDMETHOD.
```

Listing 7.3 Call of "CREATE OBJECT" Only if Instance Is Not Known Yet

You can already determine here that the constructor only needs to refresh the attributes. This is a task that the `BI_PERSISTENT~REFRESH` method can also assume. So you only need to set the key attribute in the constructor and call the `BI_PERSISTENT~REFRESH` method (see Figure 7.5 and Listing 7.4).

Ty.	Parameter	Type spec.
▸□	VALUE(ZIP_ID)	TYPE GUID_16

Figure 7.5 "constructor" Signature

```
METHOD constructor.

  me->zip_id  = zip_id.
  me->bi_persistent~refresh( ).

ENDMETHOD.
```

Listing 7.4 Constructor with Workflow Functionality

The coding for the parameter-free `BI_PERSISTENT~REFRESH` method can then call another refresh method for each more complex attribute (see Listing 7.5). Alternatively, you can call another method that refreshes all indirect (calculated) attributes.

```
METHOD bi_persistent~refresh.

  me->attrib1_refresh( ).
  me->classref_refresh( ).
  me->check_consistency( ).

ENDMETHOD.
```

Listing 7.5 Refresh Method for the Workflow Engine

In short, the `BI_PERSISTENT~REFRESH` method ensures consistency within the class and provides current attributes.

Now turn your attention to the destructive side of the class (see Listing 7.6). The Workflow Engine informs you via the parameter-free call of the `BI_OBJECT~RELEASE` method that the called class instance is no longer required and that appropriate measures must be taken to achieve a clean state in the next garbage collect.

```
METHOD bi_object~release.

  FREE  me->classref.
  CLEAR me->classref.
  CLEAR me->attrib1.

  DELETE TABLE
```

```
    zcl_wf_zip=>mst_instances[]
    WITH TABLE KEY guid = me->zip_id.

  CLEAR me->zip_id.

ENDMETHOD.
```

Listing 7.6 Removing a Class Instance

Finally, you must provide a `DELETE_INSTANCE` instance method, which in turn calls the `BI_OBJECT~RELEASE` method. You are now provided with all workflow-relevant code parts in the test environment and in the ABAP_UNIT tests. The management of instances in a static table offers the prerequisite required for high-performance behavior in the workflow environment.

But what happens if the workflow runs for a very, very long time? What if a system reset takes place between the workflow start and the work item start? Let's move to the next section to learn the answers to these questions.

7.5 The Little Persistence in Between

If a workflow runs over long periods of time, the instance management using a static table is still insufficient. This is due to the fact that if you switch off the system midway through the workflow, the static memory area of an ABAP Objects class is deleted as well. However, the Workflow Engine determines a class instance again using `FIND_BY_LPOR` after a reset or migration.

Therefore, you have no choice but to temporarily store all variables that you require for a re-instantiation of the classes you used.

Persistent classes are the first choice in the ABAP Objects environment to keep the content of attributes in sync with the content of the database. However, another approach is provided for utility classes; that is, for classes with predominately static methods and simple method interfaces. The lifetime of such classes is rarely longer than the runtime of the workflow. During the development phase, you can achieve some independence from the database design by incorporating the `IF_SERIALIZABLE_OBJECT` interface.

This is a *tagging* interface, which doesn't require any attributes or methods. It identifies an ABAP Objects class as *serializable* toward the SAP system. If you provide an

ABAP Objects class with this interface, you can convert it into an XML presentation using the standard XSLT transformation `ID` and—even better—import it again.

1. First, create a database table (which can include deep structures) for your package that contains the workflow-relevant ABAP Objects classes.

   To do so, copy the definition of the standard table INDX to your namespace in Transaction SE11, and link this table with your package (here, ZWF_XML_INDX).

2. Because the `XSTRING` data type is not readily suited for deep structures, create a table type based on the `RAW1024` ABAP line types (see Figure 7.6).

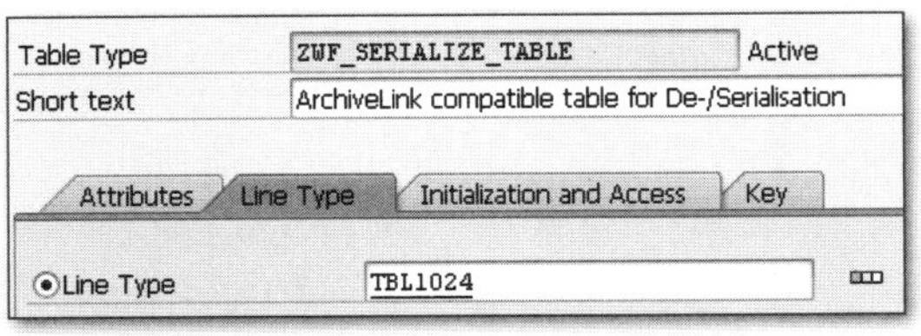

Figure 7.6 Table Type for XML Serialization

   The benefit of this data type is that you can also bypass the modules and objects of the ArchiveLink interface.

   Because you can present virtually every data type as an XML data stream and serialize every XML data stream in such a table, you can use this little detour to obtain a persistence layer that is almost general and available during prototyping.

3. Now create a DDIC structure, which connects the serialized XML data stream as a table with the key or the GUID of your workflow class. In this example it is ZWF_ZIP_STORE (see Figure 7.7).

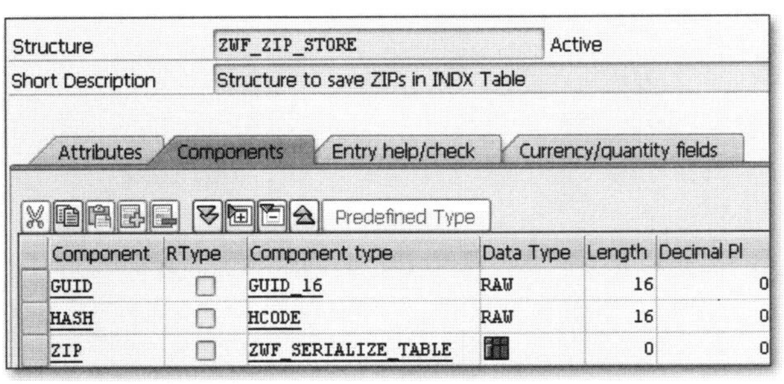

Figure 7.7 Deep Structure for Cluster Storage

The only disadvantage of this approach is that the key for the data cluster must not be longer than 22 characters. Here again, it is a good idea to work with GUIDs: You have the option to present the 16 bytes of a GUID not only as a 32-digit hexadecimal chain, but also as a 22-digit character string.

Here again, the GUID_CREATE and GUID_CONVERT modules are useful. In more recent systems, these modules were replaced by the CL_SYSTEM_UUID class, which provides static methods for creating and converting GUIDs (see SAP Note 935047, Creating GUIDs). This considerably simplifies the (de)serialization in a data cluster.

The XSLT transformation ID (identity mapping), which is predefined by SAP, is used. It is available to all ABAP Objects classes that have the IF_SERIALIZABLE_OBJECT interface, and it forms an XML string from the attributes of an ABAP Objects class. To save it in the data cluster, enter a GUID converted to 22 characters as the key.

Listing 7.7 shows an example of a SERIALIZE method, which converts "itself," that is, the ME class instance, into an XML string. This XML string is then written to your deep structure and subsequently stored in the data cluster under the ID zip_id_22. This special form of the GUID that is to be stored as a private attribute can be calculated with every refresh of the attributes, using the GUID_CONVERT function module.

```
METHOD serialize_in_table.

  DATA: oref_xml
            TYPE REF TO cl_xml_document,
        iref_xml
            TYPE REF TO if_ixml_document,
        zip_store
            TYPE  zwf_zip_store,
        l_size
            TYPE  sytabix,
        l_retcode
            TYPE  sysubrc.

* Create empty XML object
  CREATE OBJECT oref_xml.
  oref_xml->create_empty_document( ).

* Determine work interface for XML
  iref_xml = oref_xml->m_document.
```

```
* We make an XML from ourselves
  CALL TRANSFORMATION id
     SOURCE     object = me
     RESULT XML iref_xml.

* Write XML object into RAW table
  CALL METHOD oref_xml->render_2_table
    IMPORTING
      retcode = l_retcode
      table   = zip_store-zip
      size    = l_size.

* Fill deep structure with key
  zip_store-guid = me->zip_id.
  zip_store-hash = me->hash.

* Store deep structure in data cluster
  EXPORT zi = zip_store
      TO DATABASE zwf_xml_indx(zi)
      ID          zip_id_22.

ENDMETHOD.
```

Listing 7.7 Instance Method "SERIALIZE" in the Data Cluster

A static `DESERIALIZE` method (see Figure 7.8) can then work as detailed in Listing 7.8.

Ty.	Parameter	Type spec.
▸▫	VALUE(ZIP_ID_22)	TYPE GUID_22
▫	VALUE(RE_ZIP_CLASS)	TYPE REF TO ZCL_WF_ZIP

Figure 7.8 Signature for "deserialize_from_table"

```
METHOD deserialze_from_table.

  DATA: oref_xml
           TYPE REF TO cl_xml_document,
        iref_xml
           TYPE REF TO if_ixml_document,

      zip_store TYPE zwf_zip_store,
      l_size    TYPE sytabix,
```

```
      l_retcode TYPE  sysubrc.

* Read deep structure from cluster
  IMPORT zi = zip_store
       FROM DATABASE zwf_xml_indx(zi)
       ID            zip_id_22.

* Read XML object from RAW table
  CREATE OBJECT oref_xml.
  l_retcode = oref_xml->parse_table(
              table = zip_store-zip
              ).

* Determine work  interface for XML
  iref_xml = oref_xml->m_document.

* Restore data range of an ABAP-OO
* object from XML
  CALL TRANSFORMATION id
       SOURCE XML iref_xml
       RESULT object = re_zip_class.

* Restore consistency because
* transformation CONSTRUCTOR does not call
 re_zip_class->bi_persistent~refresh( ).

ENDMETHOD.
```

Listing 7.8 Static "DESERIALIZE" from Data Cluster

Don't forget to delete, which is rather trivial in this case (see Listing 7.9).

```
method DELETE_IN_TABLE.

   DELETE
     FROM DATABASE zwf_xml_indx(zi)
     ID            zip_id_22.

endmethod.
```

Listing 7.9 Deleting the Persistence in the Data Cluster

At the end of the development process, you only need to change your SERIALIZE, DESERIALIZE, and DELETE methods to work with the "real" persistent table world in your application.

7.6 Troubleshooting with Exception Classes

As an ABAP Objects programmer, you've presumably used class-based exceptions for a long time already. Let's first take a look at the exception classes that start with the abbreviation CX_BO_*. They are all derived from the abstract exception class CX_BO_APPLICATION.

If you want to use BOR objects and handle their exceptions, you can use a TRY-CATCH block on the CX_BO_APPLICATION exception class to catch all workflow-relevant exceptions. Figure 7.9 illustrates the hierarchy of these exception classes.

We already recommended that you create derived subclasses for exception handling that inherit either from the CX_BO_ERROR class or from CX_BO_TEMPORARY. This enables you to add your own error messages to the workflow log.

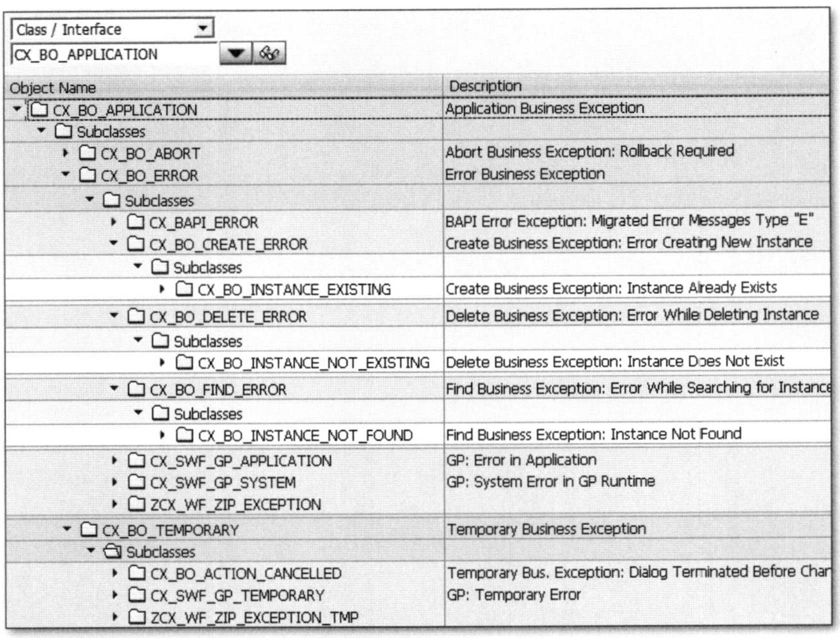

Figure 7.9 Tree of Class-Based Errors in the Workflow Context

The CX_BO_ERROR exception class and its subclasses cause the Workflow Engine to identify a work item and the associated workflow as incorrect and inform the administrator about this error.

In this context, the CX_BO_INSTANCE_NOT_FOUND exception class should be mentioned as a special case. You can trigger this exception if you encounter problems in the instance management or in the persistence layer.

You can restart such incorrect workflows using Transaction SWPR. However, such a restart must be considered in modeling so that no errors (for instance, database duplicates) result when already executed parts of a workflow template are repeated.

The CX_BO_TEMPORARY exception class indicates to the Workflow Engine that the situation is serious but not hopeless. Such a temporary error behaves differently in dialog and background work items.

- **Dialog work item**
  For a dialog work item, the temporary error is logged, and the work item is returned to the SAP Business Workplace. It may work later.

  A typical situation would be that a transaction is temporarily locked or was canceled by the employee using the CANCEL button for whatever reason. The CX_BO_ACTION_CANCELLED exception class is provided for this special case.
- **Background work item**
  For a background work item, the Workflow Engine repeatedly attempts to execute the work item. You specify in the customizing of the background job for incorrect work items (Transaction SWU3) how many failed attempts are permitted here. If the maximum number of failed attempts is reached, the workflow is handled as if the CX_BO_ERROR exception class was triggered.

Your workflow-like ABAP Objects class should be "error-tolerant" to such an extent that these two main error causes are sufficient enough to describe you error situation. All higher-level error management should be handled in the workflow-template. For example, if you trigger the CX_BO_ABORT exception class, the Workflow Engine assumes an inconsistent database world. This condition is critical because a workflow should be above the transactional context. Reconsider your object design in this case.

You should not report further exception situations to the Workflow Engine by creating an exception class, but you should catch them appropriately in your development. Usually, you can indicate exceptions through internal ABAP Objects events and handle them within the ABAP Objects class.

To inform the workflow about special situations nevertheless, we recommend using real workflow events in the handling method for internal ABAP Objects events. This is illustrated in the following section.

7.7 Creating Workflow Events from ABAP Objects Classes

In an ABAP Objects development, critical status changes, for instance, CHANGED or DELETED, are indicated by ABAP Objects events within the class.

These ABAP Objects events must be modeled because they can carry parameters. Additionally, you must define at least one method as the event handler for this event. The parameters of this method must match the parameters of the ABAP Objects event. This method is then registered at the runtime of the class for the ABAP Objects event.

Figure 7.10 illustrates how to define an ABAP Objects event as CHANGED.

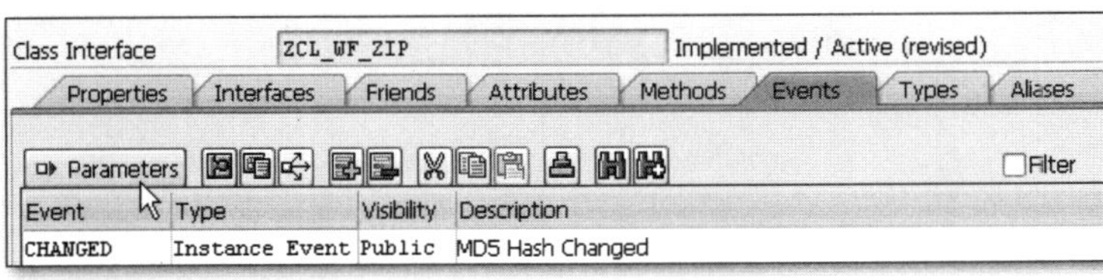

Figure 7.10 Defining an ABAP Objects Event

You implicitly define the import parameters of the method, which acts as the event handler, based on the parameters for this ABAP Objects event (see Figure 7.11).

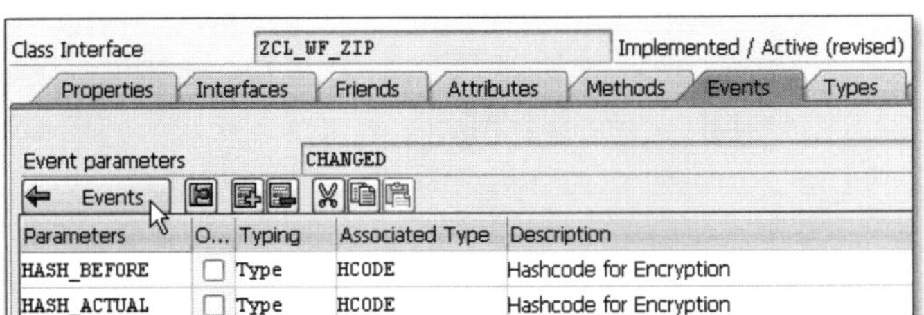

Figure 7.11 Fixed Parameter Typing also for ABAP Objects Events

As you've probably already guessed, you are supposed to create an ABAP Objects event in this example whenever the checksum of a zip file changes. You then use this ABAP Objects event to be used to create a workflow event.

1. First, create a `CHANGED_HANDLER` instance method including the parameters required to handle the event (see Figure 7.12).

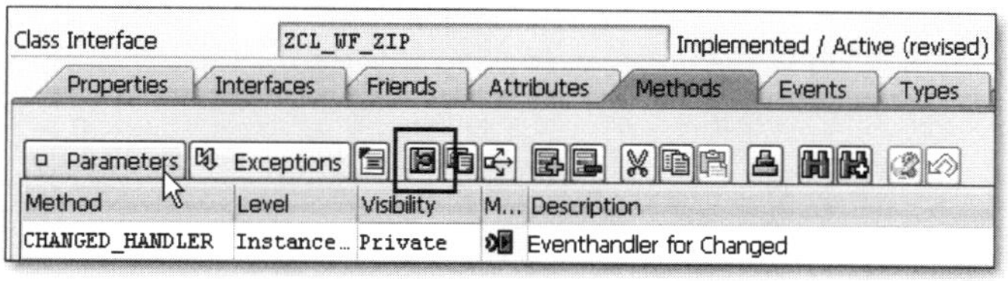

Figure 7.12 Method for Event Handling

2. To ensure that this method is defined as an event handler (icon in the METHOD TYPE column), click the DETAILS icon () to go to the detailed view of the method, where you enter the ABAP Objects event to be handled (see Figure 7.13).

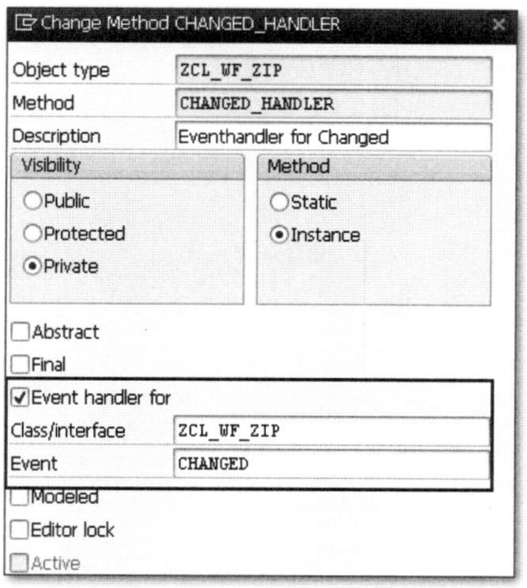

Figure 7.13 Declaring the Method as an Event Handler

3. In addition to declaring the event handler at definition time, you must register it in the `CONSTRUCTOR` method and as described in Listing 7.10 after recovery from the persistence.

```
SET HANDLER me->changed_handler FOR me.
```

Listing 7.10 Register Event Handler for an Instance at Runtime

It is a matter of taste and almost a philosophic question whether you create workflow events via instance-dependent events to have easier access to key attributes, or whether you use static events that you must provide with the key attributes in the parameter set of the event each time.

Listing 7.11 shows an example of how to create and fill an event container of the Workflow Engine and the methodology for creating a "real" workflow event.

```
METHOD changed_handler.

  CONSTANTS:
       lc_event     TYPE   sibfevent
                    VALUE  'CHANGED',
       lc_objtype   TYPE   sibftypeid
                    VALUE  'ZCL_WF_ZIP'.

  DATA:
   lv_objkey TYPE sibfinstid,
   lo_event  TYPE REF TO
         if_swf_evt_event,
   lo_evt_params TYPE REF TO
         if_swf_ifs_parameter_container.

  lv_objkey = me->zip_id.

  TRY.
     lo_event =
      cl_swf_evt_event=>get_instance(
       im_objcateg =
        cl_swf_evt_event=>mc_objcateg_cl
       im_objtype  = lc_objtype
       im_event    = lc_event
       im_objkey   = lv_objkey ).

     lo_evt_params =
       lo_event->get_event_container( ).
     lo_evt_params->set(
       name = 'HASH_BEFORE'
       value = hash_before ).
     lo_evt_params->set(
       name = 'HASH_ACTUAL'
       value = hash_actual ).
     lo_event->raise( ).
```

```
    CATCH cx_swf_evt_exception.
    CATCH cx_swf_cnt_container.
  ENDTRY.

ENDMETHOD.
```

Listing 7.11 Creating a Workflow Event in an ABAP Objects Event Handler

7.8 BOR Objects as Attributes in ABAP Objects Classes

Because the library of workflow-compliant objects in the classic environment has grown extensively, it would be a waste to leave this functionality unused and implement it anew in ABAP Objects using the workflow functionality provided by SAP.

You are frequently required to use BOR objects in "modern" ABAP Objects classes, and thus build a new functionality on existing code.

As already mentioned, BOR objects employ a somewhat different philosophy of instance creation and a different key field length. However, you still want to ensure that BOR objects can be attributes of ABAP Objects classes and vice versa.

The workflow tools in particular, such as the binding editor and the condition editor, can only tell by the defined data type that a normal ABAP Objects attribute is a BOR object. `SIBFLPORB` is the data type that indicates a reference to a BOR object to the Workflow Engine. This is simply a normal LPOR structure with a longer key (70 characters instead of 32).

You must define the specific BOR object type as a constant using a little trick. Tools like the binding editor then know exactly which BOR object type a field references—and without instantiating the ABAP Objects class. You can imagine that a couple of things happen in the background when the Workflow Engine needs to process a workflow text with the following structure:

```
&BOR_Object1.OO-Class1.BOR_Object2.OO-Class2.ATTRIBUTE&.
```

Here it is assumed that you want to place the BOR object `USR01` as an attribute in your ABAP Objects class. To inform the workflow tools that the object is of the `BO` category of the `USR01` type, you need to create a global class in the package that provides these constants.

By using a global class, you are independent of the type groups, via which you otherwise usually provide constants. But because the object is to be used by everyone without the user of the object having to enter special information in the coding, let's follow the path of the global class.

You create the `ZCL_WF_BOR_TYPES` class that includes the necessary constants for all BOR object types that you want to use as an attribute in the ABAP Objects classes.

1. Create a `public` constant of the `SIBFLPORB` type in the `ZCL_WF_BOR_TYPES` class, and edit this constant by clicking the DIRECT TYPE ENTRY icon ( ) (see Figure 7.14).

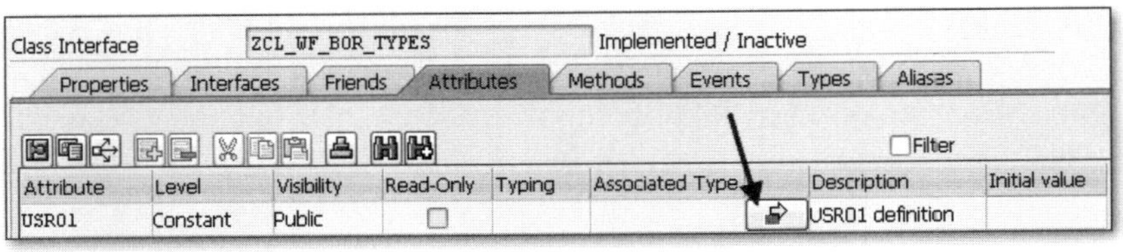

Figure 7.14 Creating a Public Constant for BOR Attributes

2. Change the type definition for the `USR01` constant as shown in Listing 7.12:

```
********  BEFORE
*  constants USR01 type SIBFLPORB .

********  AFTER
   constants:
     begin of USR01,
       instid type SIBFLPORB-INSTID value SPACE,
       typeid type SIBFLPORB-TYPEID value 'USR01',
       catid  type SIBFLPORB-CATID  value 'BO',
     end of USR01.
```

Listing 7.12 Structure Constant for the "USR01" BOR Object

3. After you save and activate the class, you can use this semifinished structure as the initial value for a BOR object or as an attribute in an ABAP Objects class. When you go back to your workflow-compatible ABAP Objects class, you can define the attributes as illustrated in Figure 7.15.

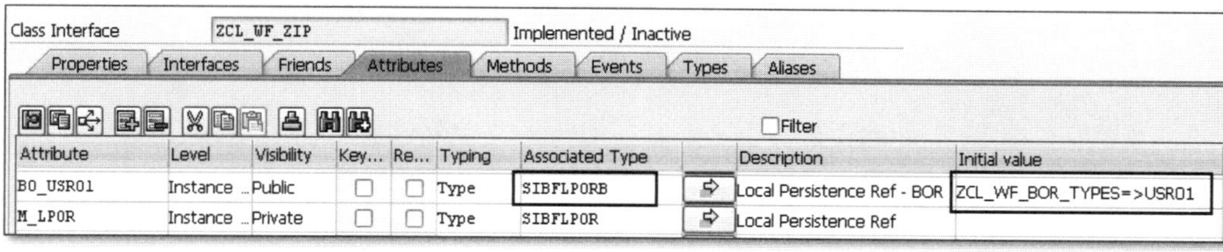

Figure 7.15 Using the Structure Constant as the Initial Value

SAP uses this technique to define the BOR object type as a constant (see the CL_SWF_BOR_TYPES class).

You then only need to set the INSTID component of the SIBFLPORB structure in the constructor of an ABAP Objects class that uses a BOR attribute. The remaining information is taken from the initial value and is enough to provide the binding editor and condition editor with sufficient details on the BOR object type that is supposed to be displayed in the editor.

8 Sample Project—Designing a BOR Object for the Workflow

SAP BusinessObjects Repository objects, which we will refer to as BOR objects, represent the technology of bundling business functionality that was originally implemented together with the Workflow Engine. The library of standard BOR objects is comprehensive and versatile. This chapter shows how to create a BOR object.

We will show you how to expand the existing SAP functionality and bundle it in a BOR object for usage in a workflow. In the course of this exercise, you will create a classic BOR object for handling zip files.

You will also learn about the development of BOR methods, the procedure for troubleshooting, and the declaration of events based on an existing functionality.

8.1 Initial Situation

In this sample project, you create a BOR object that provides the functionality of the ABAP Objects class for zip files (`CL_ABAP_ZIP`).

The SAP BusinessObjects Repository (BOR) is aging, simply because it follows a very early object-oriented approach. SAP recommends implementing new functionality with ABAP Objects if possible. But because many BOR objects are provided in the standard version, you cannot and must not ignore this "free collection of functionality." The goal of the following sections is to illustrate the most essential steps of BOR development for you, as an ABAP-experienced programmer. However, the description of the functionality of this sample project is not as detailed as in the previous chapter.

Here again, a zip file is supposed to be edited, and files are to be moved via SAP GUI upload and SAP GUI download from and to the zip file. The zip file itself is to be persisted. In other words, it is supposed to be written to the database with reference to the BOR object key. The database entries that are created within the scope of this persistence are to be removed later.

The functionality for handling the zip file is implemented with various function modules within a function group. These function modules are to be integrated with a BOR object, which will then be available to the Workflow Engine.

The BOR object bundles the functionality of this function module instance-dependently. In other words, all main parameters of the controlled function module are to be derived uniquely based on a unique key. This unique key is a character string (CHAR-like) up to 70 characters long in the BOR environment. The Workflow Engine uses the SIBFLPORB structure internally.

Frequently, a structure is defined that handles the compiled key values as an overall key. You only need to observe here that all elements of this structure must be character strings (that is, CHAR-like).

The philosophy of BOR objects assumes that for each BOR object a leading table exists where you can search the correct row with the overall key via the ABAP command SELECT SINGLE. The other columns of the row selected this way can then be copied to the BOR object as an attribute. If you refer to a custom table, the BOR editor generates a proposal for a coding that provides the row found in a structure.

The Workflow Engine assumes that the functionality used in the BOR object ensures a consistent table world itself. So regarding the Workflow Engine, it is sufficient to only keep the key and some status information between two workflow steps to reinstantiate a BOR object after a system stop or before the next workflow step.

In this sample project, the business functionality is provided by the ABAP Objects class CL_ABAP_ZIP for handling zip files or by the ABAP Objects class CL_XML_DOCUMENT for handling XML files. Accompanying the CL_XML_DOCUMENT class, a classic BOR object exists for the workflow (XML_DOC). A certain persistence can be created using the methods, save, get_doc_id, and load_from_id. This should be sufficient for the purposes of this example.

8.2 Creating a New BOR Object

Use Transaction SWO1 (Business Object Builder) to create a new BOR object. Select the Y or Z namespace as the name. Figure 8.1 shows the procedure in Transaction SWO1 for a new object ZZ_ZIPFILE.

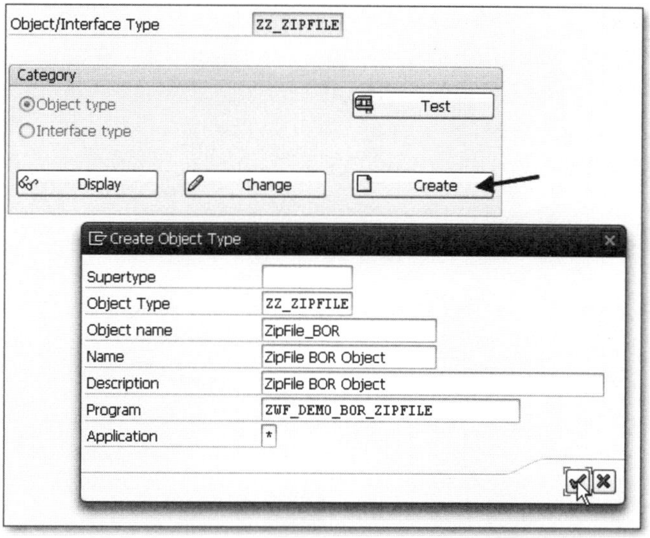

Figure 8.1 Transaction SWO1—Creating a New BOR Object for Zip Files in the Workflow

This creates a new program that you must assign to your development package, which you use for your examples. Then Transaction SWO1 looks like the screen shown in Figure 8.2.

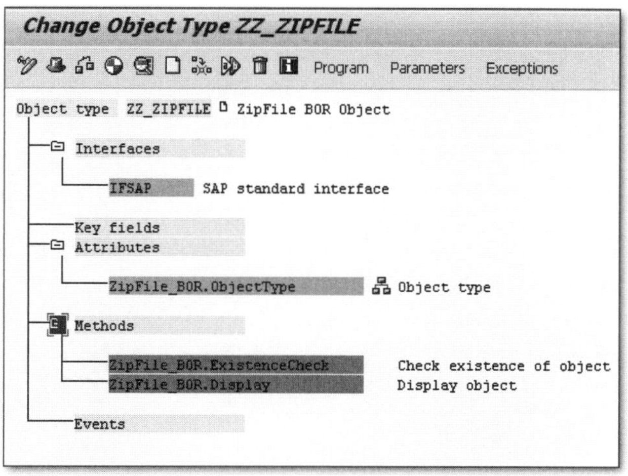

Figure 8.2 New BOR Object with "IFSAP" Interface

As you can see, the mandatory `IFSAP` interface, which requires the `ExistenceCheck` and `Display` methods, was already added.

There are additional BOR interfaces, which you can and should use for the implementation of the "typical" functionality. It is a good practice to implement at least the IFCREATE, IFDELETE, IFAUTH, and IFFIND interfaces as well. Note that you can define a default coding in interfaces with respect to the ABAP Objects philosophy. In more recent terminology, the integration of a BOR interface matches the inheritance of an abstract class.

8.3 Creating Persistence for BOR Attributes

The BOR object hierarchy assumes that you persist the workflow objects in SAP database tables by default. This is not surprising because the BOR system was integrated with the SAP system long before ABAP Objects classes, XML standards, and persistent classes.

The easiest way to work with BOR objects is if you've already created database tables where the attributes exist as columns that you want to use in the BOR object.

Because a BOR object doesn't support any structures as attributes, structured attributes must be presented via BOR objects again. As you can see here, the hierarchy of BOR objects should be very similar to the database model.

Structured Attributes in BOR Objects are BOR Objects

Note that structures are not possible as attributes.

The hierarchy of BOR objects must match the hierarchy in the database model as closely as possible. Your work is useless if you deviate from this model. In the ideal case, a simple SELECT SINGLE command with the overall key results in all necessary attributes for each BOR object. For example, separate the PURCHASE ORDER object from the PURCHASE ORDER ITEM object in your object model, and implement the item list of a purchase order as a multiline attribute with BOR objects of the PURCHASE ORDER ITEM type.

Solve model problems where they arise, that is, in the database. Ensure that your BOR object philosophy is identical with database views as much as possible.

Create a database table as an overview for the zip file.

Your table is to include one row for each file in the zip file. The GUIDs (Globally Unique Identifiers) of the zip files, which are managed by the application, only need to be registered here so that you can delete them again later on. Save the MD5 cross total (Message Digest 5) of the zip file as an additional attribute to achieve a check option for the memory content. The table will then look like the ZZZIPINFO table shown in Figure 8.3.

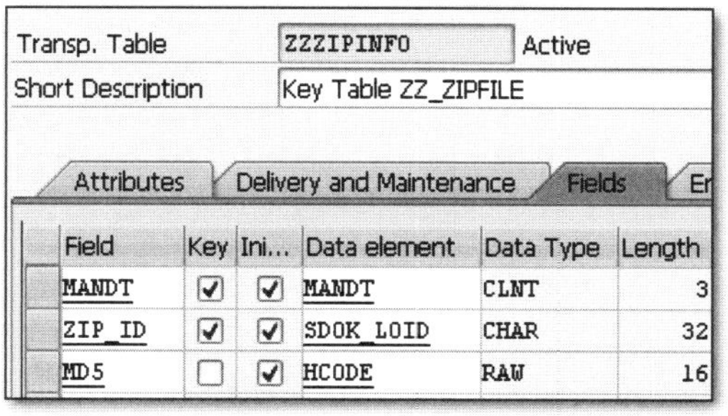

Figure 8.3 Possible INFO Table for the Sample Project

You will also use the key of the BOR object `XML_DOC` as the key for the newly created BOR object `ZZ_ZIPFILE`. In the additional ZZZIPINFO table, you only register which of the persisted XML objects the zip file from your application contains.

8.4 Creating Key and Other Attributes

The Workflow Engine can access the attributes for a BOR object. These attributes are always visible (that is, public). The attributes that contribute to the key are managed in the KEY FIELDS area in a specific way.

Return to Transaction SWO1 and first create a key attribute in the BOR object `ZZ_ZIPFILE`. To do this, proceed as follows:

1. Select KEY FIELDS and click the CREATE icon ( ) (see Figure 8.4).

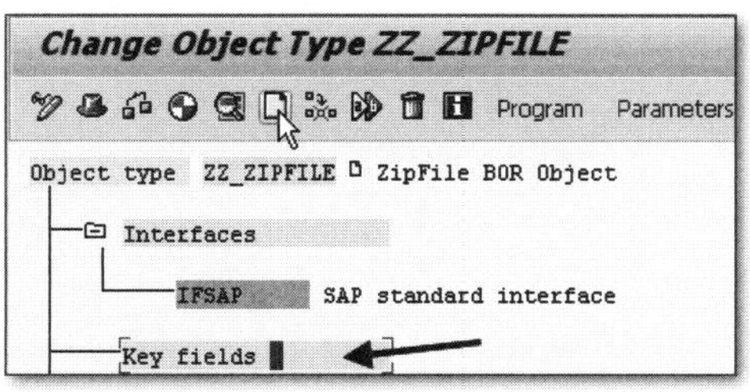

Figure 8.4 Transaction SWO1—Creating New Elements

The system displays a dialog and asks whether you want to use dictionary field specifications for the attribute.

- If you select "Yes," you can copy the definition of a column in an active database table.
- If you select "No," you have advanced setting options, which we describe in more detail later (see the step "Create second attribute" in the following).

Initially, select "Yes" here.

2. Enter "ZZZIPINFO" as the table and select the ZIP_ID field as the key field.
3. Enter "ZIP_ID" as the name of the key attribute (see Figure 8.5).

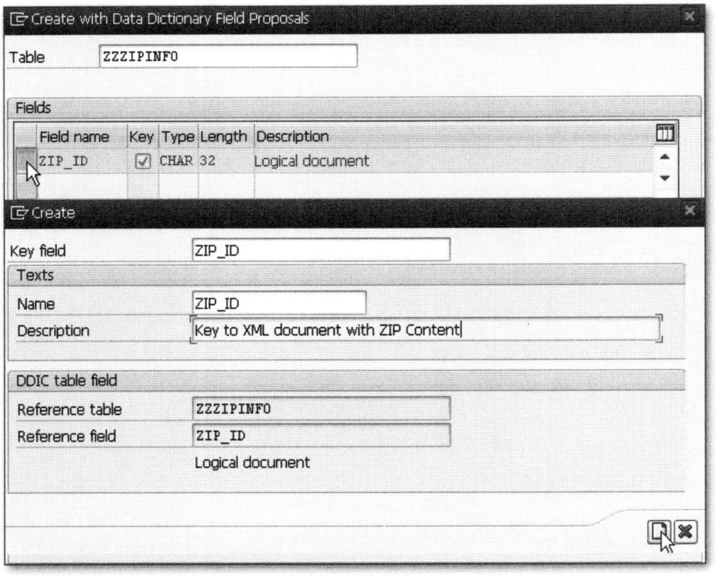

Figure 8.5 Attribute with Field Specifications from a Table

You've just created a key attribute. Now create three attributes.

- **Create first attribute**
  Create the `MD5` attribute:
  - Click in the ATTRIBUTES area and click the CREATE icon (🗋).
  - Answer the question about the field specifications with YES.
  - Then create an attribute based on the reference field (database column) MD5 in the ZZZIPINFO reference table (see Figure 8.6).

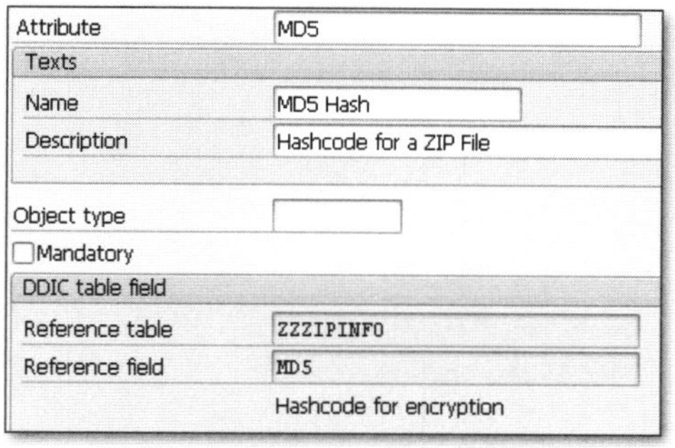

Figure 8.6 Database-Based Attribute

- **Create second attribute**
  Create the ZIP_XML attribute:
  - Click in the ATTRIBUTES area and select the CREATE icon ( ).
  - Answer the question about the field specifications with NO. Create a virtual attribute, ZIP_XML, which refers to a BOR object of the XML_DOC type (see Figure 8.7).

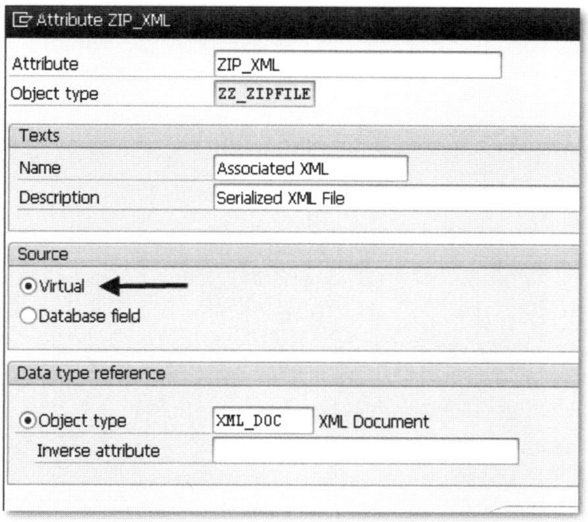

Figure 8.7 Virtual Attribute as a BOR Object Reference

- **Create third attribute**
  For the third attribute you provide the number of files in the zip file as a virtual attribute. This information comes from the CL_ABAP_ZIP class as a normal integer (in whole numbers, TYPE I). But because you require a data type reference, you must refer to the existing data type.

Note: Reference to Standard Data Types

It is important not to hastily pick a reference to a standard data field (for instance, the SYST-INDEX field). This would lead to a loss of context to the associated development package and your attribute.

The correct approach is to maintain a structure for all attributes that are not mapped in the database. This disciplinary measure is important for the transport and translations later on.

You should therefore create a DDIC structure with all fields that you may want to provide as virtual attributes and that you don't have in your database (see Figure 8.8).

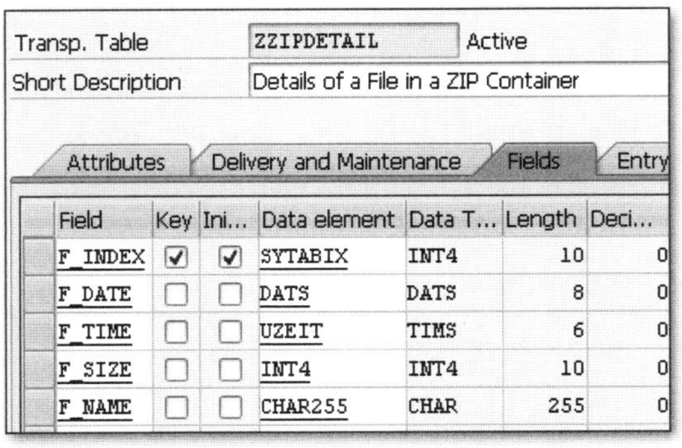

Transp. Table: ZZIPDETAIL Active
Short Description: Details of a File in a ZIP Container
Tabs: Attributes | Delivery and Maintenance | Fields | Entry

Field	Key	Ini...	Data element	Data T...	Length	Deci...
F_INDEX	☑	☑	SYTABIX	INT4	10	0
F_DATE	☐	☐	DATS	DATS	8	0
F_TIME	☐	☐	UZEIT	TIMS	6	0
F_SIZE	☐	☐	INT4	INT4	10	0
F_NAME	☐	☐	CHAR255	CHAR	255	0

Figure 8.8 DDIC Structure as the Type Reference for Potential Virtual Attributes

You can now create the third attribute:

- Click in the ATTRIBUTES area and select the CREATE icon ( ).
- Answer the question about the field specifications with NO.
- Create a virtual attribute, `FilesInZip`, that refers to an INT4-typed field of an ABAP structure in your package. This involves the ZZIPDETAIL-F_INDEX field (see Figure 8.9).

Go back to the object's overview, successively choose the key attribute and each of the three new attributes, and click the PROGRAM button (see Figure 8.10). SAP then creates a sample code for these attributes, which you must supplement later on.

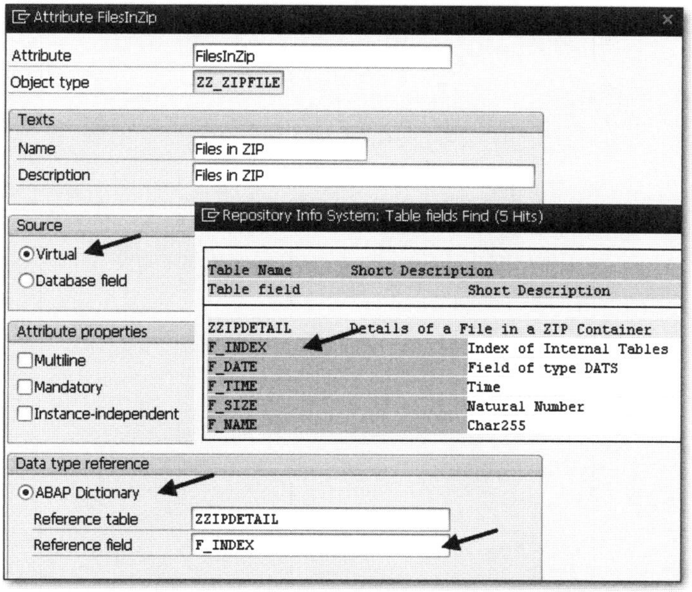

Figure 8.9 Virtual Attribute Based on a DDIC Structure Field

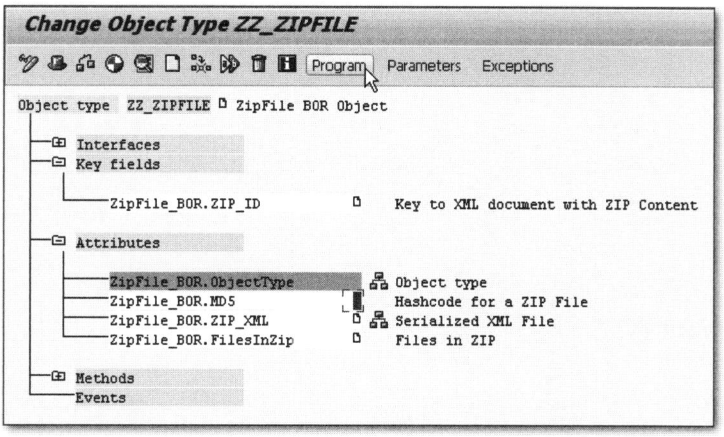

Figure 8.10 Navigating to the Program Editor of a BOR Object

The system takes you to a variant of the old R/3 ABAP editor. Unfortunately, you must work with this rather inconvenient editor here. Another disadvantage is that the generator for the sample code has never been integrated with the more recent editor in Transaction SE80. Don't try to change this part of the coding in another SAP editor.

Let's assume that SAP wants to get workflow developers to use as little coding as possible in the BOR object as a basic principle. Therefore, keep the coding in these program parts short, and call function modules or ABAP Objects methods as quickly as possible.

Listing 8.1 shows excerpts of the coding as the BOR editor generates it. Pay special attention to the bold `private` area, where you want to create private attributes, and the `SELECT` statement in the automatically generated `FROM` routine, where you must complete the `WHERE` statement manually.

```
INCLUDE <OBJECT>.

BEGIN_DATA OBJECT. " Do not change.. DATA is generated
* only private members may be inserted into structure private
DATA:
"  begin of private,
"   to declare private attributes remove comments and
"   insert private attributes here ...
"  end of private,
  BEGIN OF KEY,
      ZIP_ID LIKE ZZZIPINFO-ZIP_ID,
  END OF KEY,
      ZIP_XML TYPE SWC_OBJECT,
      FILESINZIP TYPE SYST-INDEX,
      _ZZZIPINFO LIKE ZZZIPINFO.
END_DATA OBJECT. " Do not change.. DATA is generated

TABLES ZZZIPINFO.
*
GET_TABLE_PROPERTY ZZZIPINFO.
DATA SUBRC LIKE SY-SUBRC.
* Fill TABLES ZZZIPINFO to enable Object Manager Access to Table
* Properties
  PERFORM SELECT_TABLE_ZZZIPINFO USING SUBRC.
  IF SUBRC NE 0.
    EXIT_OBJECT_NOT_FOUND.
  ENDIF.
END_PROPERTY.
*
* Use Form also for other(virtual) Properties to fill TABLES ZZZIPINFO
FORM SELECT_TABLE_ZZZIPINFO USING SUBRC LIKE SY-SUBRC.
* Select single * from ZZZIPINFO, if OBJECT-_ZZZIPINFO is initial
```

```
  IF OBJECT-_ZZZIPINFO-MANDT IS INITIAL
  AND OBJECT-_ZZZIPINFO-ZIP_ID IS INITIAL.
    SELECT SINGLE * FROM ZZZIPINFO CLIENT SPECIFIED
        WHERE MANDT = SY-MANDT
        AND ZIP_ID = ??????????.
    SUBRC = SY-SUBRC.
    IF SUBRC NE 0. EXIT. ENDIF.
    OBJECT-_ZZZIPINFO = ZZZIPINFO.
  ELSE.
    SUBRC = 0.
    ZZZIPINFO = OBJECT-_ZZZIPINFO.
  ENDIF.
ENDFORM.
```

Listing 8.1 Generated Code of the BOR Editor

Take a look at the area between `BEGIN_DATA OBJECT` and `END_DATA OBJECT`. An `OBJECT-KEY-<key field>` data field exists for each key attribute. A buffer variable `OBJECT-<VirtualAttribute>` exists for each virtual attribute. And a buffer variable `OBJECT-_<table>` is available for every table referenced by the database attribute.

The object manager in the BOR object tries to occupy the database as little as possible and reads the attributes of a BOR object from the `OBJECT` buffer area. In case of changes to the database, you must declare this buffer area as invalid using the `SWC_REFRESH_OBJECT` macro so that the table row is reread.

Now change the `private` area and the `SELECT` statement as shown in Listing 8.2. You must add the object references for the ABAP Objects classes that you require in the methods to the `private` area.

```
**** PRIVATE area
  begin of private,
"   to declare private attributes remove comments and
"   insert private attributes here ...
    m_zip      type ref to cl_abap_zip,
    m_document type ref to cl_xml_document,
  end of private,

**** SELECT statement
    SELECT SINGLE * FROM ZZZIPINFO CLIENT SPECIFIED
        WHERE MANDT = SY-MANDT
        AND ZIP_ID = OBJECT-KEY-ZIP_ID.
```

Listing 8.2 Modifications in the Generated Code

All subareas of the BOR object are still indicated as modeled, but the program code should still pass the first syntax check.

You run the syntax check in the BOR objects by clicking the CHECK icon (). The error list is available via GOTO • ERROR LIST or GOTO • NEXT ERROR.

Creating Coding for BOR Attributes

The automatically generated coding is not ready for use yet and must be supplemented.

The code generator creates GET_PROPERTY- areas in the BOR coding for each attribute. The generator's proposal for your object-like attribute ZIP_XML only contains the SWC_SET_ELEMENT macro with which the container variable is supposed to be set. Supplement the code proposal with the bold area in Listing 8.3. You can use the SWC_CREATE_OBJECT macro to create a reference to a BOR object, whose name you specify as the parameter.

```
GET_PROPERTY ZIP_XML CHANGING CONTAINER.
SWC_CREATE_OBJECT
     OBJECT-ZIP_XML 'XML_DOC'
                    OBJECT-KEY-ZIP_ID.
SWC_SET_ELEMENT CONTAINER
                'ZIP_XML'
                OBJECT-ZIP_XML.
END_PROPERTY.
```

Listing 8.3 Assigning BOR Objects to an Attribute

For the virtual attribute FilesInZip you require an ABAP Objects class reference from the private area. This area is set in the ExistenceCheck method. You must therefore always check object references in the private area for their validity with the ABAP command IS BOUND before you use them. If these reference variables are not valid, call the BOR method ExistenceCheck again (see Listing 8.4).

```
GET_PROPERTY FILESINZIP CHANGING CONTAINER.

SWC_CONTAINER emptycont.

IF NOT OBJECT-PRIVATE-M_ZIP IS BOUND.
 SWC_CALL_METHOD self
      'ExistenceCheck' emptycont.
```

```
ENDIF.

  DESCRIBE TABLE OBJECT-PRIVATE-M_ZIP->FILES[]
           LINES OBJECT-FILESINZIP.

  SWC_SET_ELEMENT CONTAINER 'FilesInZip' OBJECT-FILESINZIP.

END_PROPERTY.
```

Listing 8.4 Virtual Attribute Depending on the Class Variables

Note the `self` object reference. This reference is available in every BOR object program and can be used to deploy "own" attributes or methods.

> **Memory Aid: Procedure when Working with the BOR Editor**
>
> Remember the following with regard to the typical procedure when using the old BOR editor:
>
> - Create the key attributes. Define them using a single leading database table.
> - Define a database attribute. Then have the system generate the access routine for the database table.
> - Next, define additional—also virtual—attributes.
> - Specify all export and import parameters and the exceptions of a method. This way you obtain a better solution for the method implementation.

8.5 Creating BOR Methods

The `ExistenceCheck` method plays a special role in the methods of a BOR object. It is called implicitly whenever references to a BOR object are created using the `SWC_CREATE_OBJECT` macro.

Picture the `ExistenceCheck` method as some kind of post-constructor method for BOR objects. Provided that you use ABAP Objects classes, like we do in this example, you must "redefine" the default coding, which is provided by the `IFSAP` interface. To do this, proceed as follows:

1. Click the `ExistenceCheck` method and click the REDEFINE button (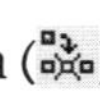) (see Figure 8.11).

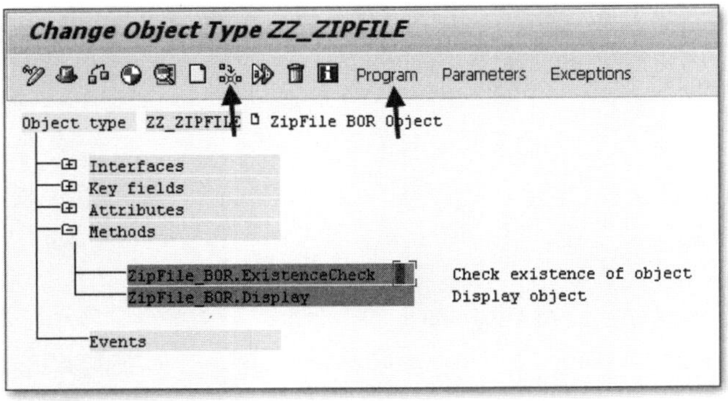

Figure 8.11 Redefining the "ExistenceCheck" Method

2. Then click the PROGRAM button (see Figures 8.10 and 8.11) and change the `ExistenceCheck` method in such a way that all necessary variables are set in the `private` area of the object (see Figure 8.5, earlier in this chapter).
3. Ensure that the buffer row of your key table is filled with current values. If there are no hits based on the key specified or if you suspect that the key value in the `OBJECT-KEY` variable is invalid, inform the BOR object manager about the nonexistence of this object at runtime by calling the `EXIT_OBJECT_NOT_FOUND` macro.

   The source code in the `ExistenceCheck` method should look as shown in Listing 8.5.

```
BEGIN_METHOD EXISTENCECHECK CHANGING CONTAINER.

DATA SUBRC LIKE SY-SUBRC.

 PERFORM SELECT_TABLE_ZZZIPINFO USING SUBRC.
  IF SUBRC NE 0.
    EXIT_OBJECT_NOT_FOUND.
  ENDIF.

****Trigger business logic and
****fill OBJECT-PRIVATE

CALL FUNCTION 'ZWF_BORZIP_LOAD_OR_CREATE'
 EXPORTING
   XML_ID              = OBJECT-KEY-ZIP_ID
   CREATE_FLAG         = ' '
IMPORTING
```

```
    XMLREF              = OBJECT-PRIVATE-M_DOCUMENT
    ZIPREF              = OBJECT-PRIVATE-M_ZIP
EXCEPTIONS
    NOT_FOUND           = 1
    XML_ERROR           = 2
    OTHERS              = 3.
IF sy-subrc <> 0.
  EXIT_OBJECT_NOT_FOUND.
ENDIF.

END_METHOD.
```

Listing 8.5 Possible Source Code for the "ExistenceCheck" Method

Implementing the `ExistenceCheck` method is one of the most important steps on the way to an executable BOR object.

8.5.1 Additional BOR Interfaces

As already mentioned, it is useful to integrate additional standard BOR interfaces. To do this, proceed as follows:

1. In Transaction SWO1, click in the INTERFACES area and click the CREATE icon (□).
2. Add the standard interfaces `IFCREATE` and `IFDELETE`. You thus add two additional methods marked in red that you must redefine.

8.5.2 Redefining the "CREATE" Method

Because a default coding "brought along" by an interface is not exactly useful for your application, you now "redefine" the default coding.

In Transaction SWO1 (see Figure 8.1), proceed as follows:

1. Select the `CREATE` method and select the REDEFINE method (icon).
2. Now double-click the `Create` method, which is now displayed in white.
3. Maintain the details as shown in Figure 8.12. In doing so, you inform the system that the `Create` method is instance-independent (static) and thus returns a BOR object reference to the ZZ_ZIPFILE object type.

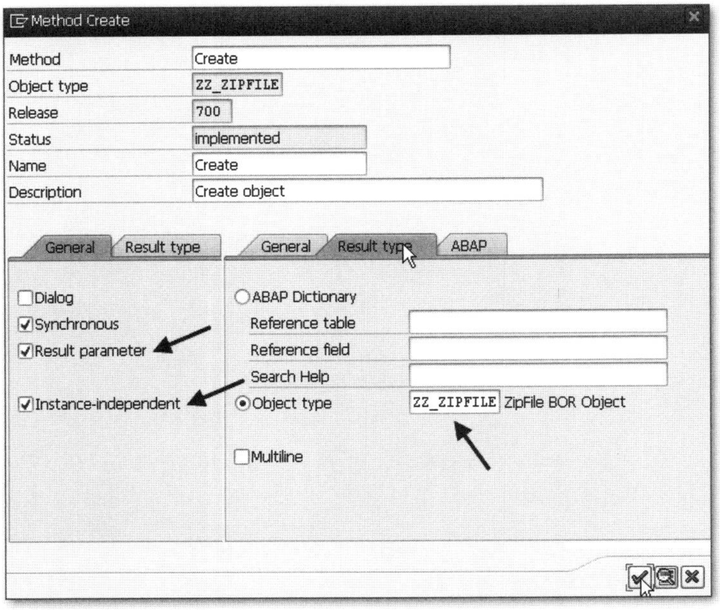

Figure 8.12 "CREATE" Method as an Instance-Independent Method with Object Type as the Result Parameter

`CREATE` is an instance-independent method. It is therefore similar to a `public static` method in the ABAP Objects environment. It is common practice to extend the `CREATE` method to a factory method (instance creation method) that returns an instance of the BOR object as the result parameter. This factory method can be used within the SAP test scope.

8.5.3 Method Containers for Parameters

All parameters of a BOR method are transferred in a container. Parameters are also to be transferred to the `CREATE` method. Within the coding for the method, you must retrieve any parameters from the method container. Define the structure of this method container first. Proceed as follows:

1. Select the `Create` method, and then click the PARAMETERS button.
2. Define an import and an export parameter, `XML_ID`, as shown in Figure 8.13. Click BACK () to exit the maintenance page. The save option only exists on the overview page for the BOR object.

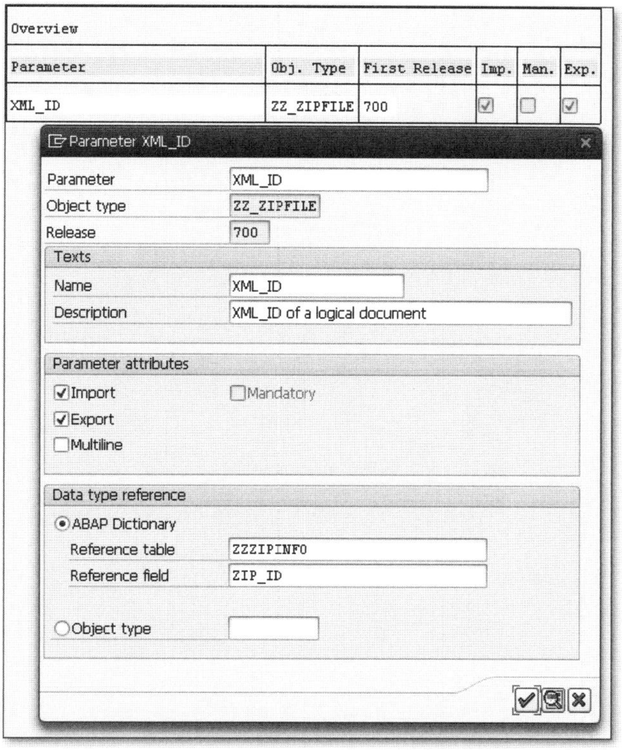

Figure 8.13 Defining an Entry in a Method Container

Note that the result parameter does not appear in this overview of the method container; it is predefined under the name `RESULT` and must be set explicitly using the macros `SWC_SET_ELEMENT` or `SWC_SET_TABLE` (if multiline).

Listing 8.6 shows a possible source code for the `Create` method. This example shows that you should quickly call a function module with the actual functionality. For this purpose, use `SWC_GET_ELEMENT` to retrieve parameters from the method container. The actual functionality is then executed, and variables of the BOR object from the `OBJECT-PRIVATE` structure are also available. Any errors are sent to the Workflow Engine using the `EXIT_RETURN` macro. Ultimately, the export parameters and the special result parameter `RESULT` are returned to the method container.

```
BEGIN_METHOD CREATE CHANGING CONTAINER.

DATA:  l_xml_id type  SDOK_LOID,
       l_return_obj type SWC_OBJECT.
```

```
SWC_GET_ELEMENT CONTAINER 'xml_id' l_xml_id .

CALL FUNCTION 'ZWF_BORZIP_LOAD_OR_CREATE'
 EXPORTING
   XML_ID          = l_xml_id
   CREATE_FLAG     = 'X'
   DISPLAY_XML     = ' '
 IMPORTING
   XMLREF          = OBJECT-PRIVATE-M_DOCUMENT
   ZIPREF          = OBJECT-PRIVATE-M_ZIP
   E_XML_ID        = l_xml_id
 EXCEPTIONS
   NOT_FOUND       = 1
   XML_ERROR       = 2
   OTHERS          = 3.
IF sy-subrc <> 0.
SWC_SET_ELEMENT CONTAINER 'xml_id' space.

EXIT_RETURN 0001 space space space space.

ELSE.
   SWC_SET_ELEMENT CONTAINER 'xml_id' l_xml_id.
   swc_set_objectkey l_xml_id.
   SWC_CREATE_OBJECT l_return_obj 'ZZ_ZIPFILE' l_xml_id.
   SWC_SET_ELEMENT
           CONTAINER
           RESULT l_return_obj.
ENDIF.
```

Listing 8.6 Handling the Parameter Container and Setting the "RESULT" Element in the "CREATE" Example

8.5.4 Redefining the "DELETE" Method

The DELETE method, which you copied by incorporating the BOR interface IFDELETE, contains a default code. This code uses the EXIT_NOT_IMPLEMENTED macro to inform you that the local implementation is still missing (see Listing 8.7).

```
BEGIN_METHOD DELETE CHANGING CONTAINER.
* local implementation doesn't exist
  EXIT_NOT_IMPLEMENTED 'Delete'.
END_METHOD.
```

Listing 8.7 "EXIT_NOT_IMPLEMENTED" Macro in the Default Code of Interfaces

This illustrates how an interface can include a default coding. However, this default coding is to be replaced by a more suitable source code.

For this purpose, select the `DELETE` method and click the REDEFINE button. Listing 8.8 shows the basic idea of a `DELETE` method:

```
BEGIN_METHOD DELETE CHANGING CONTAINER.


CALL FUNCTION 'ZWF_BORZIP_DELETE_ZIP'
  EXPORTING
    xml_id    = OBJECT-KEY-ZIP_ID
  CHANGING
    xmlref    = OBJECT-PRIVATE-M_DOCUMENT
    zipref    = OBJECT-PRIVATE-M_ZIP
 EXCEPTIONS
   NOT_FOUND        = 1
   CANCELLED        = 2
   OTHERS           = 3
          .
IF sy-subrc <> 0.
  EXIT_RETURN 9001 OBJECT-KEY-ZIP_ID
                   space
                   space
                   space.
ENDIF.

SWC_SET_OBJECTKEY SPACE.

END_METHOD.
```

Listing 8.8 Possible Coding for "DELETE"

A function module assumes the actual work. This function module is provided with key elements from the `OBJECT-KEY` structure and with private variables of the BOR object from the `OBJECT-PRIVATE` structure.

8.6 Exceptions and Errors

We've already mention the `EXIT_RETURN` macro in the last two listings. It is used for exception management in the BOR environment. The error messages created this way are displayed in the workflow log and must be defined via a message class.

For this purpose, reselect the `CREATE` method and click the Exceptions button. Exceptions and the associated message text can be transferred via interfaces (see Figure 8.14).

Exceptions

No.	Obj. Type	Temp.	Appl.	Syst.	AppAr	Message	Message Text
0001	IFCREATE	☐	☑	☐	OL	700	Object could not be created
0002	IFCREATE	☐	☑	☐	OL	813	Mandatory parameter '&' missing
0003	IFCREATE	☐	☑	☐	OL	701	Original has not yet been assigned

Figure 8.14 Exceptions from the "IFCREATE" Interface

The number range as of 9000 is available for exceptions in your development. Therefore, maintain a message class in Transaction SE91 (Message Maintenance) and assign it to your development package (for instance, `ZWF_DEMO` from Chapter 5).

1. Reselect the `DELETE` method and click the Exceptions button.
2. Then click the Create icon ( ).
3. In the following dialog, decide whether the exception to be defined is supposed to result in a temporary error or in an application error (see Figure 8.15).

You can choose up to four placeholders for variable contents in the message text (special character `&`). The values for these placeholders `&` reach the message texts as parameters of the `EXIT_RETURN` macro.

In addition, two special macros are defined for triggering an exception.

- **EXIT_OBJECT_NOT_FOUND**
  This macro, particularly in the `ExistenceCheck` method, provides the information that no instance corresponding to the key value could be found.
- **EXIT_CANCELLED**
  This macro informs the Workflow Engine that a temporary error is to be triggered with a special meaning. If the processing was canceled by a user action,

for instance, cancelation of a transaction, the workflow can respond accordingly. The relevant work item then remains in the SAP Business Workplace and can be called again.

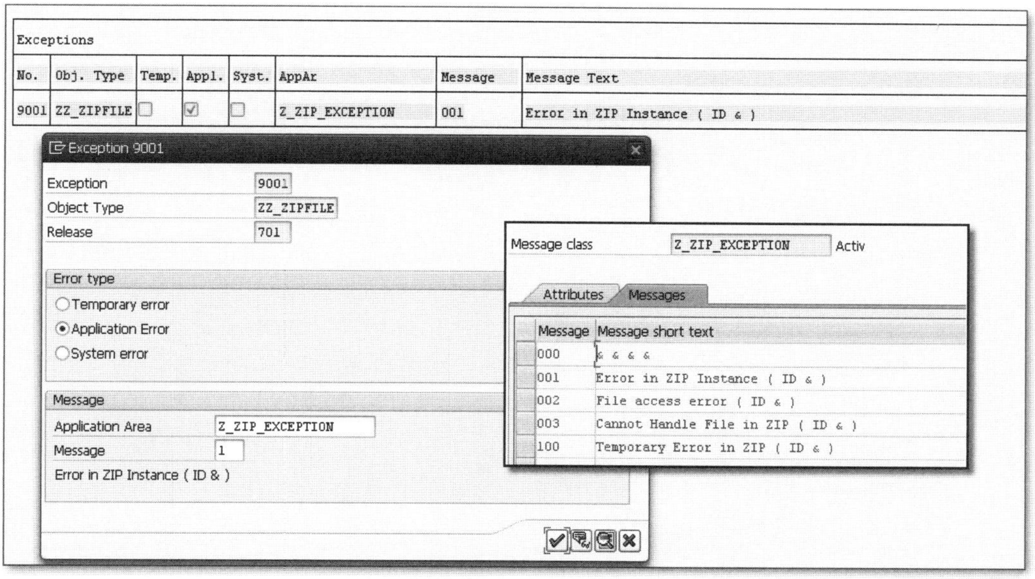

Figure 8.15 Application Error in the "DELETE" Method

8.7 BOR Events

Within Transaction SWO1 (Business Object Builder), you only need to define the permitted events and their parameters. The events themselves are then created within the business logic.

You use the `SWE_EVENT_CREATE` and `SWE_EVENT_CREATE_FOR_UPD_TASK` function modules for classic ABAP programming. You should use the event creation in the UPDATE TASK; that is, the part of the SAP system that writes to the database. The UPDATE TASK is a defined point in time during the runtime of the update task, from which the data was already written to the database. Compared with the synchronous function module `SWE_EVENT_CREATE`, the asynchronous approach with the `SWE_EVENT_CREATE_FOR_UPD_TASK` function module has the benefit that the SAP system defines the time for executing the `COMMIT WORK` command.

If you create events in BAdIs or user exits, you mix up the database contents of the surrounding application when you also call the `COMMIT WORK` command that is required for creating events.

So select an additional flag for all modules, in which you create both events. This flag specifies whether the `COMMIT WORK` command is to be executed or not. This enables you to control this command by customizing your application if required.

In your sample project, you define the events `CREATED` and `DELETED` with a parameter that is based on the SYST-UNAME field. Select the EVENTS area and create the two events by clicking the CREATE button (□).

The dialog that appears does not have any specific features except for the TRIGGERING OBJECT DOES NOT EXIST checkbox. With this checkbox you inform the Workflow Engine that it is no longer supposed to search for a runtime instance when the event is sent or create any instance because the object cannot and must not be instantiated any longer in case of `DELETED` (see Figure 8.16).

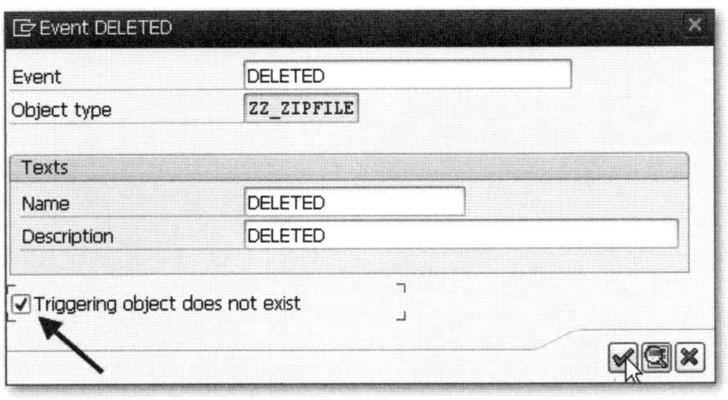

Figure 8.16 Special Checkbox for "DELETED" Events

Select the events you want to provide with parameters, and then select PARAMETERS. The definition of event parameters is similar to that of method parameters. Listing 8.9 shows the creation of a `DELETED` event via the UPDATE TASK.

```
DATA: objtype TYPE swo_objtyp,
      objkey  TYPE swo_typeid,
      event   TYPE swo_event.

 objtype  = 'ZZ_ZIPFILE'.
 objkey   = xml_id.
 event    = 'DELETED'.
```

```
swc_container   evt_container.
CLEAR evt_container.
swc_set_element evt_container 'UserName' sy-uname.

CALL FUNCTION 'SWE_EVENT_CREATE_FOR_UPD_TASK'
  EXPORTING
    objtype            = objtype
    objkey             = objkey
    event              = event
  TABLES
    event_container    = evt_container
  EXCEPTIONS
    objtype_not_found = 1
    OTHERS             = 2.
IF sy-subrc = 0 AND do_commit = 'X'.
  COMMIT WORK.
ENDIF.
```

Listing 8.9 Creating Events in the System's UPDATE TASK

8.8 BOR Release Statuses

BOR object types are supposed to represent a highly robust interface to the application functionality. You can therefore release or lock both the entire object type and the individual components, such as methods or events, for use by others. If you want to deliver workflow templates to third parties, these statuses are important for your customers.

- **"Modeled" Status**
  Components in the "Modeled" status are not visible from the outside. If you also provide your workflow developments for other systems, you should only use elements in the "Released" status.
- **"Released" Status**
  Workflow developers may use elements in the "Released" status. For BOR objects provided by SAP, you can assume that these objects are further developed with upward compatibility. Object type components can only be released if the object type is in the "Released" status.
- **"Obsolete" Status**
  You will rarely use the "Obsolete" status. SAP uses it to indicate the discontinuation

of maintenance of BOR components in the standard SAP system. If you come across this status, you should check the SAP notes (OSS notes) for comments on the discontinued support for this BOR subcomponent. Usually, these notes indicate alternatives that describe how to replace the obsolete BOR subcomponent.

- **"Implemented" Status**
  The "Implemented" status is sufficient to start the component in the development system for testing purposes. If SAP uses this status on the "standard" BOR-Objects, expect changes in the next service releases.

So before you deliver your packages, switch to the "To released" status. To change the status, access Transaction SWO1 and follow the path Edit • Change Release Status • Object Type or Edit • Change Release Status • Object Type Component (see Figure 8.17).

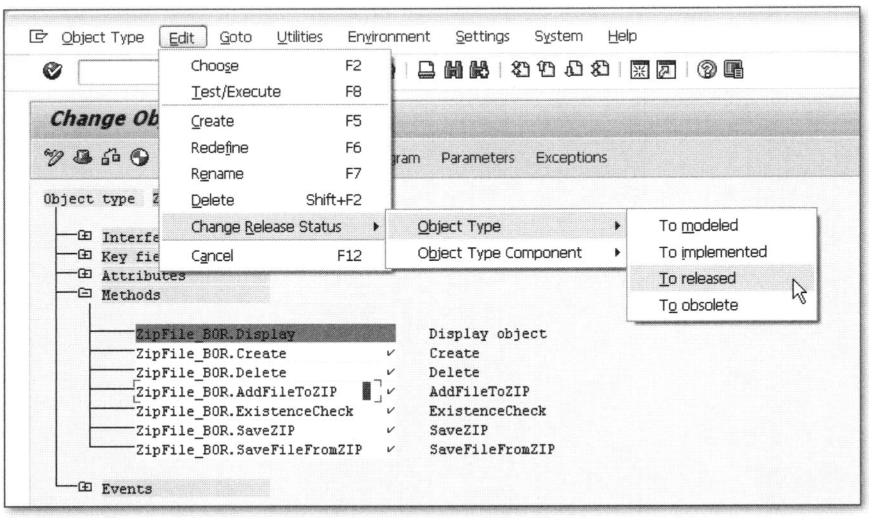

Figure 8.17 Changing the Release Status in Transaction SWO1

8.9 Default BOR Specifications

You can select one method and one attribute as the default for the Workflow Engine. These defaults are used to perform a typical action (default method, usually, "display") or create a text that identifies the BOR object (default attribute, usually a text presentation of the key BOR attributes):

- Object name
- Default method
- Default attribute

This is the *object name* that is displayed in the development environment and for maintaining container elements and bindings. This object name should be meaningful for all people involved in development. It is not translated.

The two other defaults are available via the menu option GOTO • BASIC DATA on the DEFAULTS tab (see Figure 8.18).

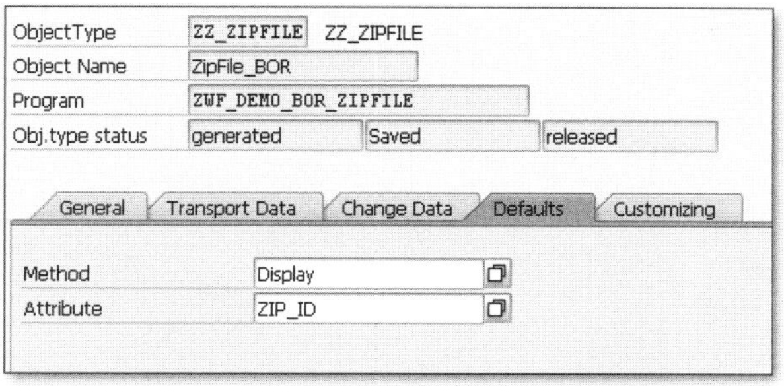

Figure 8.18 Default Method and Default Attribute

The *default method* is called whenever the user double-clicks an object link in the SAP GUI. End users usually expect the system to display something meaningful that gives more information on the object concerned. Usually, you enter the display method that opens the relevant transaction in the display mode.

The default method is called in the source code via the `SWC_CALL_METHOD` macro if `SPACE` is transferred as the method name.

The *default attribute* is displayed in lists and texts; in other words, whenever an object must be displayed as text. We recommend implementing a virtual attribute as the default attribute. The virtual attribute then provides the object name and the values of the key fields as readable text (for instance, purchase order 08154711). This enables you to optimally utilize the descriptive texts and translations from the Data Dictionary (DDIC).

The default attribute is called in the source code via the `SWC_GET_PROPER` macro if `SPACE` is transferred as the attribute name.

8.10 Inheritance and Delegation in BOR

The *inheritance* in the BOR hierarchy works more or less as an ABAP Objects developer would expect it to. When you define a BOR object, you enter a *SUPERTYPE*, which is the BOR object type whose functionality you want to inherit. The methods, attributes, and events of this SUPERTYPE are then also available in the derived objet type (the SUBTYPE) (see Figure 8.19). You can add object type components or redefine them locally.

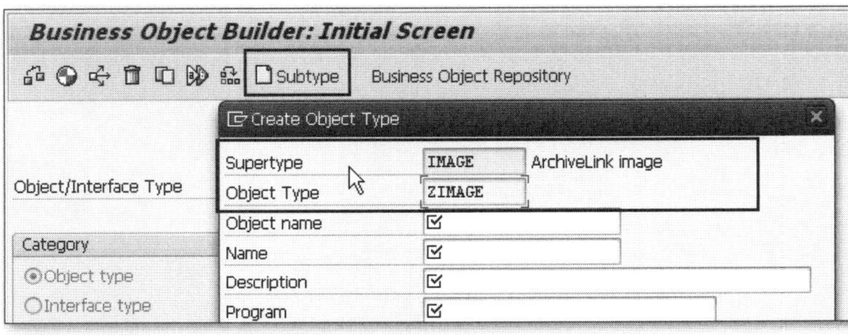

Figure 8.19 Creating a SUBTYPE for a BOR Object

The *delegation* becomes necessary when you want to "teach" a BOR object, even though this BOR object doesn't belong to your development. Let's consider an example: Say you want to supplement an SAP-provided BOR object with additional functionality without modifying it. To do so, proceed as follows:

1. If possible, add your enhancements to an interface type. Standard objects frequently lack specific events or enterprise-specific procedures for archiving or logging.
2. Define a BOR object type that is derived from the SAP BOR object. Supplement it with the interface you've developed. This way, it obtains the event definitions and a default coding for your functionality.

If the new functionality is supposed to take effect only in the workflows you've defined, the steps described so far may be sufficient. But if a standard workflow is to respond to events that you've just defined and if a seamless "casting" is to be possible between the SUPERTYPE and the derived object type, you must enter a delegation. This is possible only once per object type in the system. However, you have the option to link delegations.

Let's assume your archive provider has already delegated the ZIMAGE BOR object type to the IMAGE BOR object type to enable the recording of bar codes in all images.

If you now want to delegate additional events or methods to an IMAGE object, you must create another SUBTYPE of the ZIMAGE object type and delegate this ZZIMAGE object type to ZIMAGE so that the functionality of the first delegation is not lost.

You can maintain the delegations in Transaction SWO1 in the initial screen via SETTINGS • DELEGATION. Ensure that you don't transport delegations but have them entered manually so that no existing delegation is overwritten.

If the delegation is activated, the methods and events defined in the derived BOR object type are also available in the original object type.

A concrete example where you require a delegation would be an enhancement to the USR01 BOR object, which is included in many other BOR objects as an attribute with object value.

Assume that you want to pass a specific enterprise-internal aspect to all USR01 objects, for example, to another virtual attribute, KnownInLdap, which checks in an LDAP whether this SAP user is linked with a central user account.

If you redelegate a ZUSR01 object that is derived from the USR01 object, all USR011 objects in the system will behave as if they had had this attribute originally—even though this functionality comes from the ZUSR01 BOR object.

Appendices

A Step Types and Sample Workflows

Strictly speaking, the ABAP world is a huge open source community. That means that it is absolutely legitimate, necessary, and required to analyze the existing code in the SAP system. This also holds true for a quick start to workflow programming.

Transaction SWUI_VERIFY (Start Test Workflows) provides numerous workflow templates you can use as examples. This appendix is a brief guide, sorted by step types and other workflow technologies.

A.1 Step Types

This Essentials guide does not discuss the workflow design, but only the ABAP part of workflow programming. Nevertheless, this section provides a brief summary of possible workflow steps.

Activity

This step executes a single workflow task. You usually embed a standard task (task beginning with "TS") here that refers to a BOR method or an ABAP Objects class method.

A simple example of this step type is the sample workflow template `WF_Verify038` for BOR methods and the workflow template `WF_Verify048` for ABAP Objects classes.

Subworkflow

This step is generated as a normal activity ( ), but a workflow template (template beginning with "WS") is defined instead of a standard task. This changes the icon in the graphical Workflow Builder to .

A simple example of this step type is the sample workflow template `WF_Verify039` and the workflow template `WF_Verify020`.

Condition

This step evaluates a condition using container elements of the workflow container. This condition has two exits, TRUE and FALSE.

A simple example of this step type is the sample workflow template `WF_Verify022`.

Multiple Condition

The value of a workflow container element determines which branch in the workflow template is selected. Workflow branches don't have to be defined for every possible value. You can also use a branch for OTHER VALUES (`OTHERS`).

A simple example of this step type is the sample workflow template `WF_Verify010`.

User Decision

The SAP Business Workplace provides a list of predefined selection options. Each option corresponds to a branch in the workflow template.

You can find an example of this technology in the workflow template `WF_Verify002`.

Undefined Step

You can use an undefined step as a placeholder for future steps during development (prototyping).

You can find an example of this step type in the workflow template `WF_Verify002`.

Container Operation

The use of constants and content of the workflow container enables you to fill additional elements in the workflow container via assignments.

You can find an example of this technology in the workflow template `WF_Verify042`.

Event Creator

An event is generated. The event container is filled from the workflow container.

You can find examples of this technology in the workflow templates `WF_Verify042` and `WF_Verify043`.

Wait Step (Wait for Event)

The Workflow Engine waits to complete this step until it receives a certain event.

You can find an example of this technology in the workflow template `WF_Verify043`.

Document from Template

A document is generated from a template. During this process, specific placeholders in the text are replaced with workflow container content.

You can find an example of this technology in the workflow template `WF_Verify018`.

Fork

This workflow step enables you to generate multiple branches in the workflow template. These branches are processed in parallel. You have to define the number of parallel branches and determine how many of these branches have to be fully processed before the system closes the parallel area and continues with processing the "normal" workflow template. Alternatively, you can formulate an end condition that completes the parallel area.

Simple examples of this step type are the workflow templates `WF_Verify008` and `WF_Verify009`.

Process Control

This step enables you to manipulate the execution of a work item or an entire workflow. You can cancel work items or define them as "obsolete."

Examples of this step type include the workflow templates `WF_Verify012`, `WF_Verify013`, and `WF_Verify014`.

Loop (UNTIL/WHILE)

A step sequence is processed several times. The termination criterion is checked either at the beginning (WHILE) or at the end (UNTIL) of the loop.

You can find examples of these loop technologies in the workflow templates `WFWF_Verify023` and `WF_Verify024`.

Send Mail

The system sends the entered text as an SAP email. For sending external emails, however, further administrative SAP Basis activities need to be carried out.

You can find an example of this technology in the workflow template `WF_Verify032`.

Form

Container elements of the workflow container are displayed or entered in a form.

A simple example of this step type is the sample workflow template `WF_Verify029`.

Block

Blocks enable you to model a group of steps collectively and define deadline monitoring for the group's processing.

A rather complex example of this step type is the sample workflow template `WF_Verify050` for dynamic sequences.

You can find another complex example of exception handling in blocks in the workflow template, `WF_Verify046`.

Local Workflow

Local workflows are "free" blocks. The Workflow Builder displays them next to the actual workflow template. You start local workflows via events. You can also store them as modules in your workflow template so that you obtain a workflow design with components.

A simple example of this step type is the sample workflow template `WF_Verify042`.

Web Activity

Selected container elements are generated as XML binding and transferred to a web server. This enables you to call a SOAP Web service from the workflow.

The most obvious example of this step type is the sample workflow template `WF_Verify101`.

Ad hoc Anchor

This step type enables an authorized group of persons to intervene in a running workflow. Here, the anchor is where one of several predefined workflow templates is displayed as a subworkflow.

This is a quite complex workflow technology and makes sense only in a few revision scenarios.

A.2 Other Workflow Technologies

In addition to the individual step types, there are other frequently recurring design technologies in the workflow environment.

Parallelization Using a Multiline Element (ParForEach)

In the details view of a workflow activity in the Workflow Builder, you can implement parallel execution on the OTHER tab. The activity is executed several times via a multiline container element in the workflow container.

A simple example of this step type is the sample workflow template `WF_Verify019`.

Before, Secondary, and After Methods

When a dialog work item is executed, you can execute other activities before, after, and in parallel with this action.

A possible example of the use of secondary methods is the sample workflow template `WF_Verify026`.

Deadline Monitoring

You should implement deadline monitoring for all dialog steps in a workflow template—if the agent determination does not determine the appropriate agent or if employees are absent. If periods expire, usually supervisors or substitutes are involved in the business process as well.

Deadline monitoring options can be found in the sample workflow templates `WF_Verify000`, `WF_Verify001`, `WF_Verify004`, and `WF_Verify005`.

B Important Transactions

This appendix lists some typical questions that are asked when workflow problems occur.

- **Are there SAP runtime errors that are caused by background steps?**
  Transaction ST22 (ABAP Runtime Error). Select the runtime errors that were caused by the WF-BATCH user.
- **Does the event queue work?**
  To check, use Transactions SWE5 (Consistency Check for Event Linkages) and SWEQADM (Event Queue Administration). The event queue works if all traffic lights are green.
- **How many instances with missed deadlines and errors exist?**
  To answer this question, use Transaction SWF_GMP (Workflow Administrator Overview).
- **How many instances exist without agent?**
  To check this, use Transactions SWI2_ADM1 (Work Items without Agent) and SWI2_ADM2 (Work Items with Deleted Agents).
  - If this check determines that there are instances without agents, use Transaction SWIA (Process Work Item as Administrator) to correct the situation.
  - If you cannot resend work items, it may be necessary to remove them as the administrator using Transaction SWWL (Delete Work Items).
- **Do the background jobs of the Workflow Engine run as scheduled?**
  You can check and correct this with the following transactions:
  - SWWA (Maintain Work Item Deadline Monitoring)
  - SWWB (Re-Schedule Work Item Deadline Monitoring)
  - SWWD (Configure Work Item Error Monitoring)
  - SWU3 (Automatic Workflow Customizing)

The following tables list important transactions concerning the workflow development department:

Selection and Administration of Work Items	
SWIA	Process Work Items Administratively
SWI1	Selection via all Work Items
SWI2_DIAG	Find Incorrect Work Items
SWI2_DEAD	Work Items with Missed Deadline
SWI2_ADM1	Find Work Items without Agents
SWI2_ADM2	Work Items with Deleted Agents
SWPR	Workflow Restart After Error
SWPC	Workflow Restart After System Crash
SWWA/SWWB	Re-Schedule Workflow Background Jobs for Deadline Monitoring
SWWD	Maintain and Schedule Workflow Background Jobs for Error Monitoring
SWWL	Delete Work Items

Tools for Workflow Events	
SWU0	Simulate Events and Test Event Linkage
SWUE	Trigger Events
SWEL	Display Event Trace
SWELS	Switch Event Trace On/Off
SWEQADM	Event Queue Administration
SWEQBROWSER	Event Queue Overview
SWEC	Trigger Events via Change Documents
SWED	Link Change Documents and Object Types
SWUY	Link Workflow Creation to Messages
SWETYPV	Event Linkage for Triggering Events
SWEINST	Event Linkage for Closing Events
SWE5	Consistency Check of Event Linkage

Tools for Workflow Developers	
SWDD	Fast Access Workflow Builder
SWDD_CONFIG	Adapt Workflow Template of SAP or Third Party
SWU4	Syntax Check for Workflow Tasks
SWU7	Syntax Check for Workflow Templates
SWF_TRC	Workflow Trace
SWF_GMP	Administration Overview for Workflow Engine
SWU3	Central Automatic Customizing
SWB_COND	Start Conditions for Workflow Templates
SWUD	Topical Diagnosis of the Workflow Environment
PFTC	Access to Development Environment for Workflow Objects Except for Rules
PFAC	Access to Development Environment for Workflow Rules
SWUS	Workflow Test Environment
SWO1	Development Environment for BOR Objects
SE80	ABAP Development Environment (also for Business Engineering Objects)

Transactions for the Organizational Environment	
PPOCW	Create Organizational Structure for the Workflow
PPOMW	Process Organizational Structure for the Workflow
SWU_OBUF	Refresh Buffer of the Organizational Environment
SWLC	Check Organizational Assignment of Tasks

C The Author

Like many other physicists, **Ilja-Daniel Werner** ultimately ended up working with the topic of process optimization and interfaces. His areas of expertise comprise everything that no one sees but is still necessary for operation. He has worked in the SAP environment for more than ten years, and he designs large workflow products and enterprise projects for PSINOVA AG. He also works as a lecturer for the German-speaking SAP training centers.

Index

S

T

U

V

W

X